A-Z KINGSTON U

C000195768

CONTENTS

REFERENCE

A Road	A1034	Car Park (selected)	P
Proposed		Park & Ride	Walton St. P+🚌
B Road	B1231	Church or Chapel	†
Dual Carriageway		Cycleway	🚲
One-way Street	→	Fire Station	■
Traffic flow on A Roads is also indicated by a heavy line on the driver's left.	→	Hospital	Ⓗ
Restricted Access		House Numbers — Selected Roads	245 32
Pedestrianized Road		Information Centre	🛈
Track / Footpath		National Grid Reference	⁵05
Residential Walkway		Police Station	▲
Railway — Level Crossing — Station — Tunnel		Post Office	★
		Toilet: without facilities for the Disabled / with facilities for the Disabled / for exclusive use by the Disabled	▽ ▽ ▽
Built-up Area	VICTOR ST	Viewpoint	🔆 ☀
Local Authority Boundary	— · — · —	Educational Establishment	⌐
Posttown Boundary	———	Hospital, Hospice or Health Centre	⌐
Postcode Boundary within Posttown	— —— —	Industrial Building	⌐
		Leisure or Recreational Facility	⌐
		Place of Interest	⌐
		Public Building	⌐
Map Continuation	16 Large Scale City Centre 4	Shopping Centre or Market	⌐
		Other Selected Buildings	⌐

SCALE

Map Pages 6-59 1:15840	Map Pages 4-5 1:7920
0 ¼ ½ Mile	0 ⅛ ¼ Mile
0 250 500 750 Metres	0 100 200 300 Metres
4 inches (10.16 cm) to 1 mile 6.31 cm to 1 km	8 inches (20.32 cm) to 1 mile 12.63 cm to 1 km

Copyright of Geographers' A-Z Map Company Ltd.

Head Office:
Fairfield Road, Borough Green, Sevenoaks, Kent,
TN15 8PP
Telephone 01732 781000
(General Enquiries & Trade Sales)

Showrooms:
44 Gray's Inn Road, London, WC1X 8HX
Telephone 020 7440 9500 (Retail Sales)

www.a-zmaps.co.uk

Ordnance Survey® This product includes mapping data licensed from Ordnance Survey with the permission of the Controller of Her Majesty's Stationery Office.

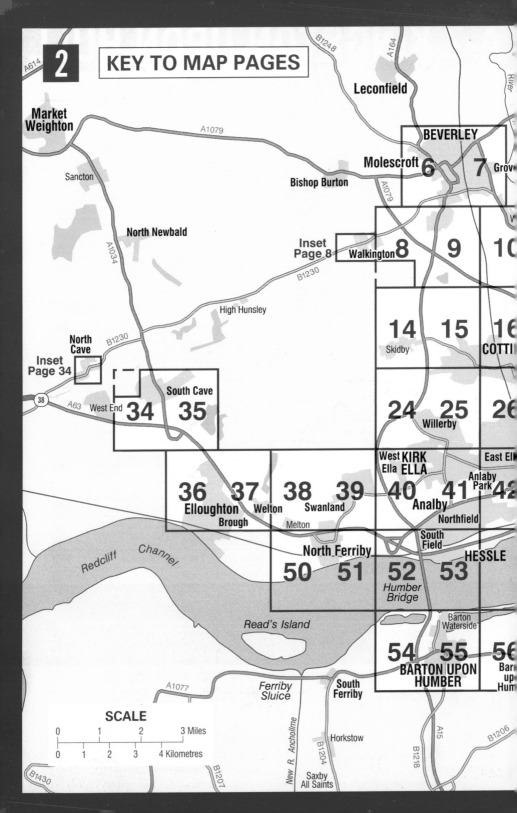

A614

A1248

A164

River

Leconfield

Market Weighton

A1079

BEVERLEY

Molescroft **6**

7 Grov

Sancton

Bishop Burton

A1079

North Newbald

Inset Page 8

Walkington **8**

9

10

W

A1034

B1230

High Hunsley

North Cave

B1230

Inset Page 34

38

A63

West End **34**

South Cave **35**

14

15

16

Skidby

COTTI

24

25

Willerby

26

West Ella **KIRK ELLA**

East Ell

Anlaby Park

42

36

37

Elloughton

Brough

Welton

38

39

Swanland

Melton

40

Analby

41

Northfield

South Field

HESSLE

Redcliff Channel

North Ferriby

50

51

52

Humber Bridge

53

Read's Island

Barton Waterside

54

55

BARTON UPON HUMBER

56

Bar up Hum

A1077

Ferriby Sluice

South Ferriby

New R. Ancholme

A15

B1206

B1218

SCALE

0   1   2   3 Miles

0   1   2   3   4 Kilometres

B1430

B1207

Horkstow

B1204

Saxby All Saints

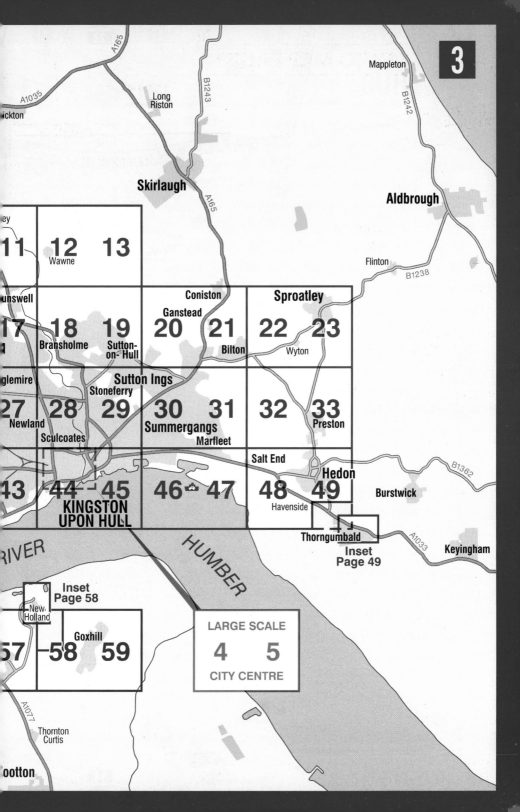

3

Mappleton

A1035
A165
B1243
Long Riston
ickton

Skirlaugh

Aldbrough
B1242

Flinton
B1238

ey
11 | **12** Wawne | **13**

unswell | **17** | **18** Bransholme | **19** Sutton-on-Hull

Coniston
Ganstead
Sproatley
20 | **21** Bilton | **22** Wyton | **23**

glemire | Sutton Ings | Stoneferry
27 | **28** Newland Sculcoates | **29** | **30** Summergangs | **31** Marfleet | **32** | **33** Preston

Salt End
Hedon
B1362
43 | **44** KINGSTON UPON HULL | **45** | **46** | **47** | **48** Havenside | **49** | Burstwick

RIVER

HUMBER

Thorngumbald
Inset Page 49
A1033
Keyingham

Inset Page 58
New Holland
57 | **58** Goxhill | **59**

LARGE SCALE
4 **5**
CITY CENTRE

A1077
Thornton Curtis

ootton

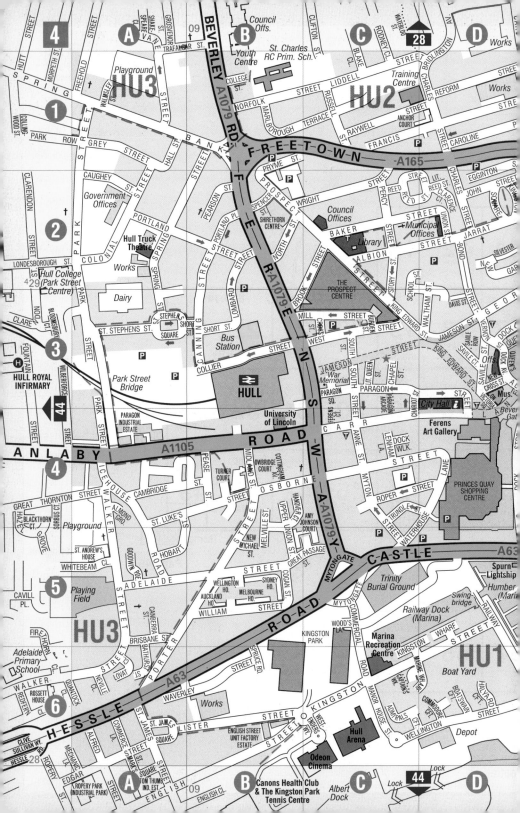

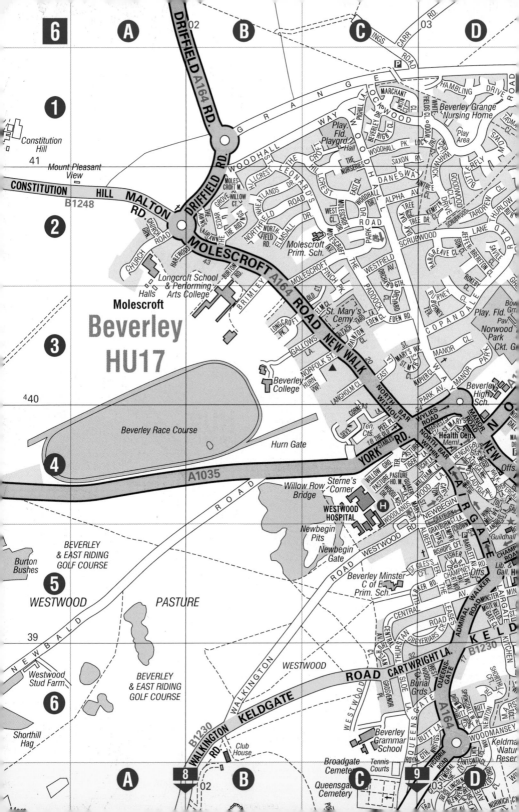

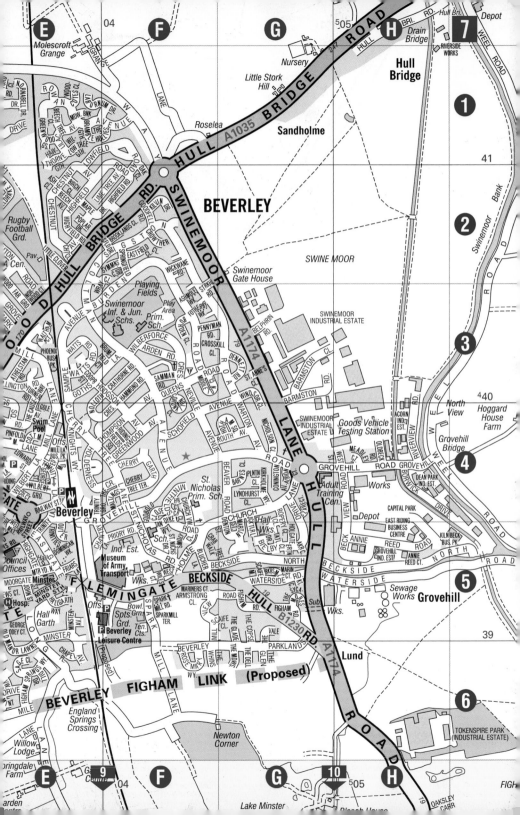

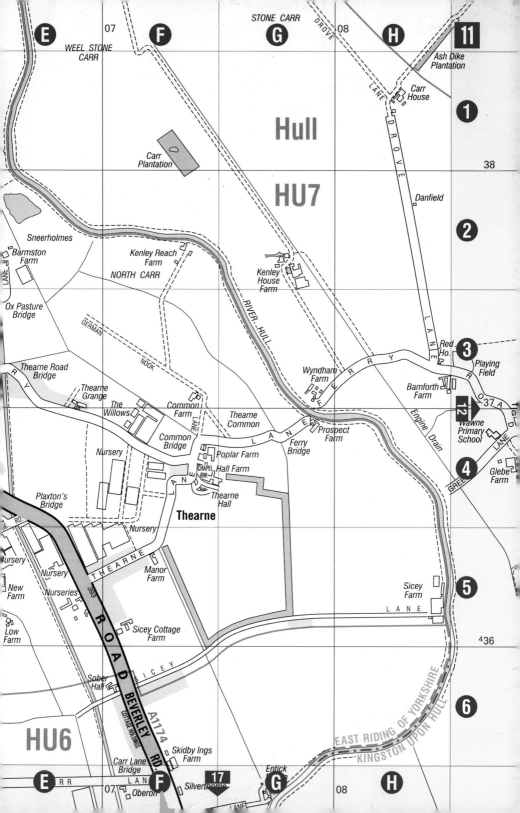

E 07 **F** STONE CARR **G** DROVE 08 **H** **11**

WEEL STONE CARR

Ash Dike Plantation

Carr House

1

Hull

Carr Plantation

38

HU7

Danfield

2

Sneerholmes

Barmston Farm

Kenley Reach Farm

NORTH CARR

Kenley House Farm

Ox Pasture Bridge

RIVER HULL

GERMAN NOOK

Red Ho.

3

Playing Field

Thearne Road Bridge

Wyndham Farm

Thearne Grange

Bamforth Farm

The Willows

Common Farm

LANE

Thearne Common

Prospect Farm

Engine Drain

Wawne Primary School

12

Common Bridge

Poplar Farm

Ferry Bridge

GREEN LANE

4

Glebe Farm

Nursery

CHAPEL RW

Hall Farm

Thearne Hall

Plaxton's Bridge

Thearne

Nursery

THEARNE

Manor Farm

Sicey Farm

5

Nursery

New Farm

393

Nurseries

LANE

Low Farm

Sicey Cottage Farm

436

EAST RIDING OF YORKSHIRE

6

HU6

SICEY RD.

Sober Hall

BEVERLEY

A1174 CUTTING-HOLDINGS

KINGSTON UPON HULL

Skidby Ings Farm

17

Entick

Carr Lane Bridge

Silverthorpe

E R R 07 **F** LANE Oberon **G** 08 **H**

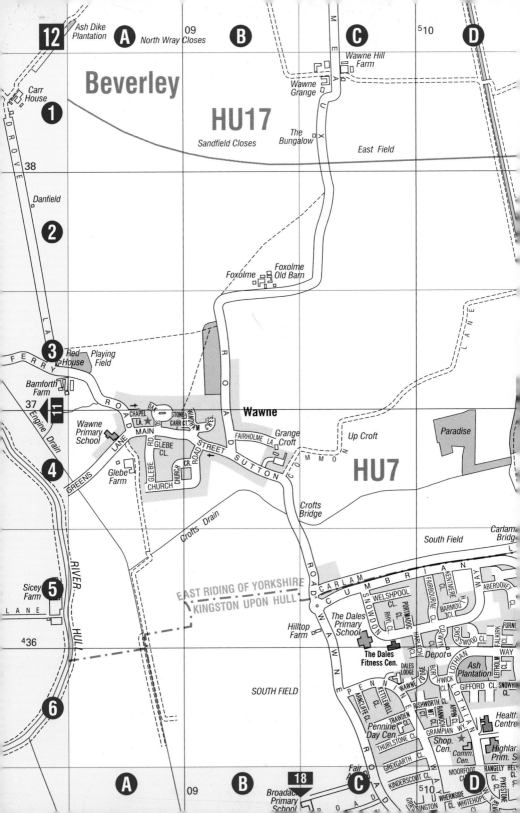

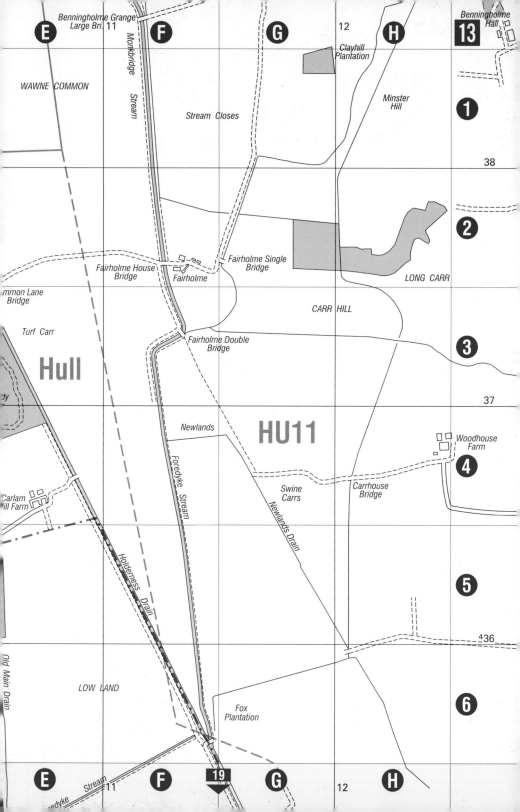

E Benningholme Grange
Large Bri. 11

F

G

12

H

Benningholme
Hall

13

WAWNE COMMON

Monkbridge Stream

Clayhill
Plantation

Minster
Hill

1

38

Stream Closes

2

LONG CARR

Fairholme Single
Bridge

Fairholme House
Bridge

Fairholme

CARR HILL

mmon Lane
Bridge

3

Turf Carr

Fairholme Double
Bridge

37

Hull

Newlands

HU11

Woodhouse
Farm

4

dy

Foredyke Stream

Swine
Carrs

Carrhouse
Bridge

Carlam
ill Farm

Newlands Drain

5

Holderness Drain

436

Old Main Drain

LOW LAND

Fox
Plantation

6

E

redyke Stream 11

F

19

G

12

H

Foredyke Stream

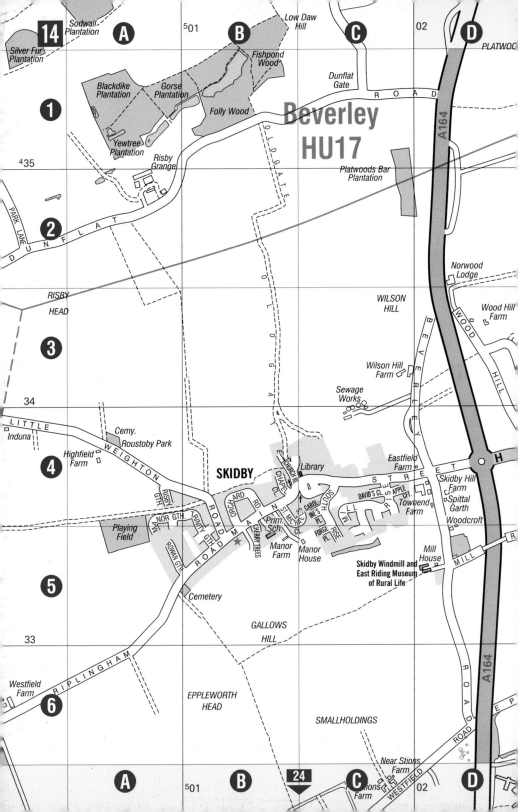

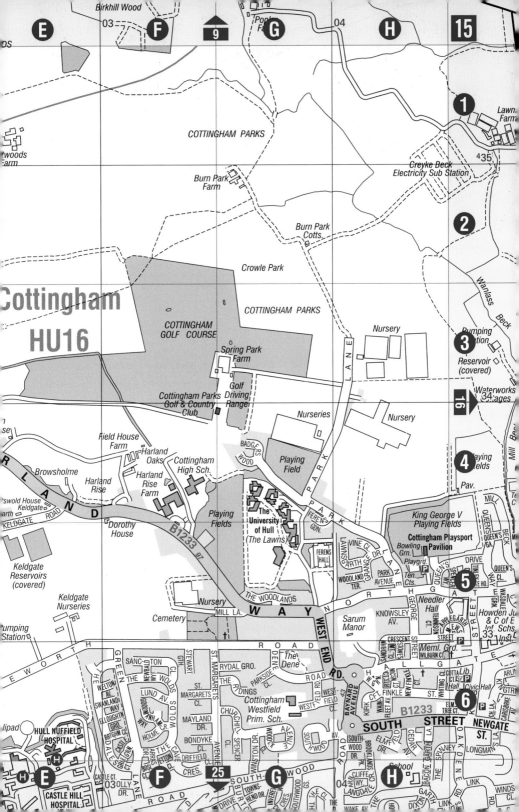

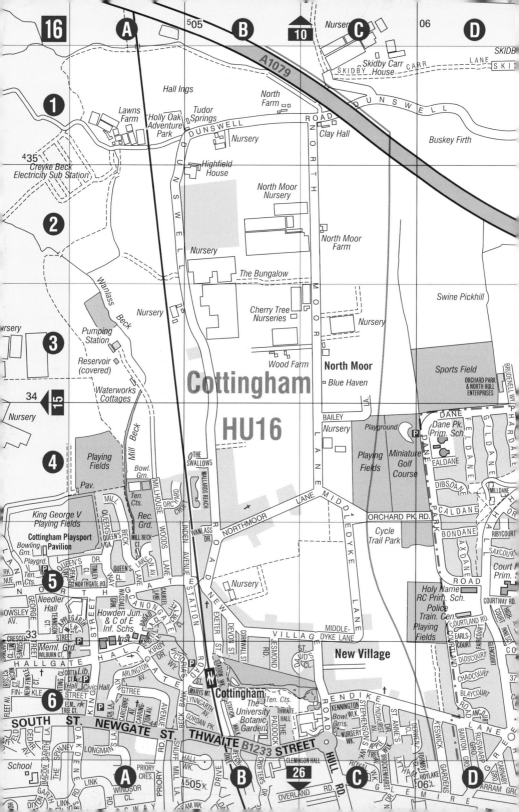

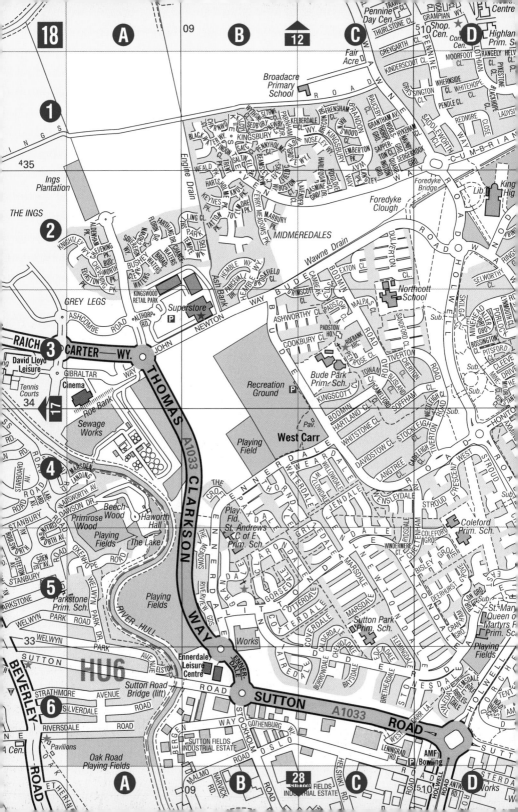

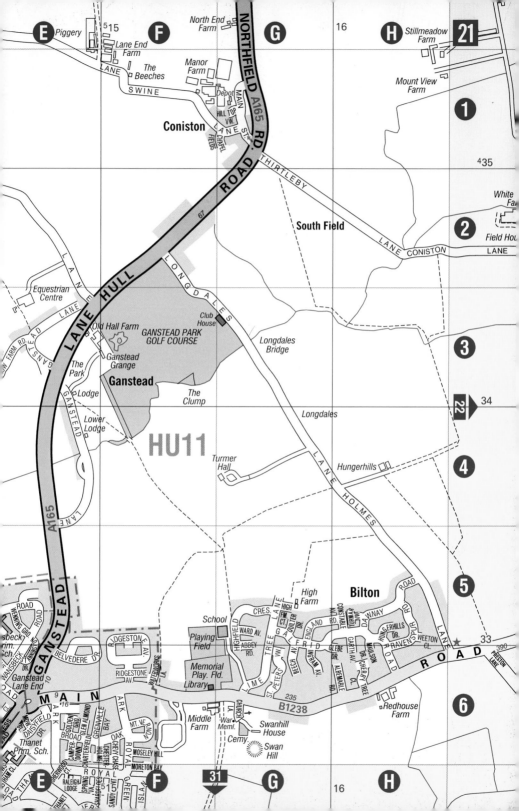

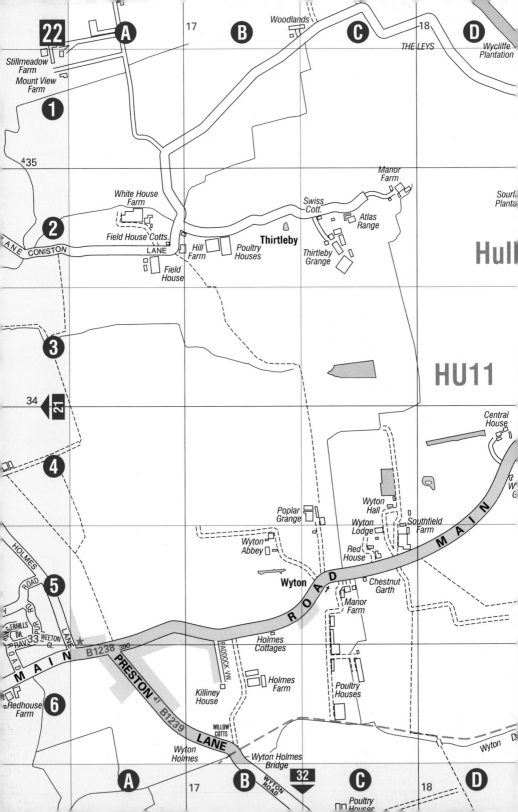

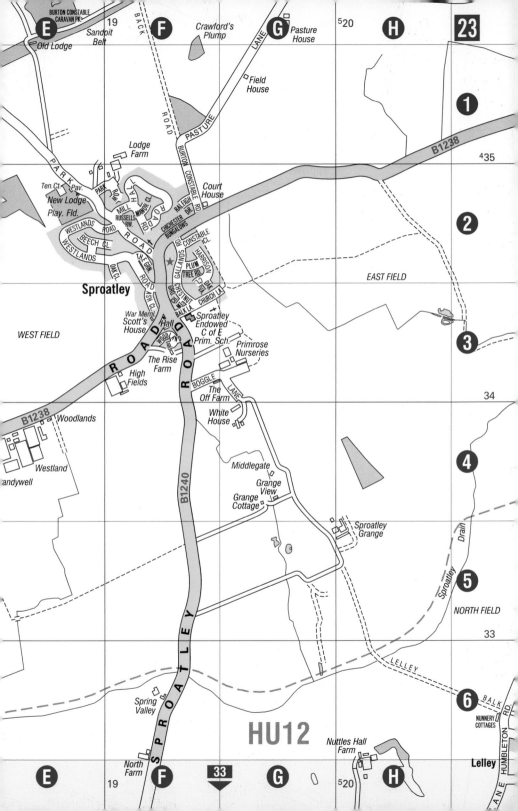

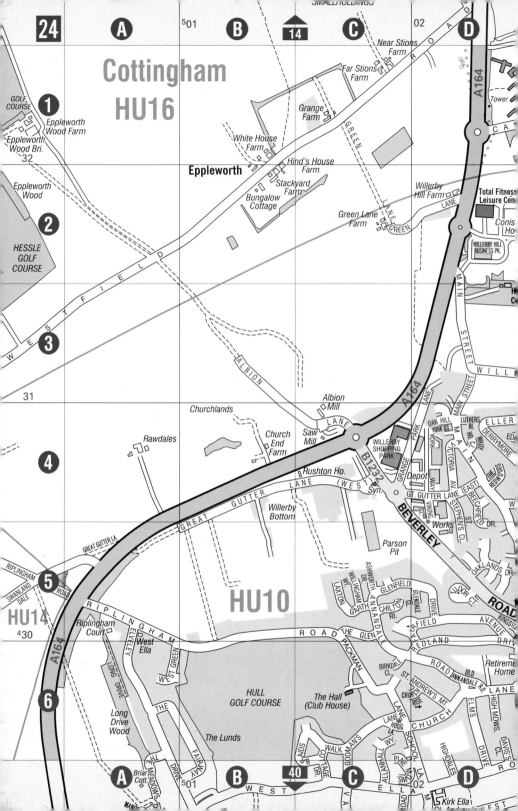

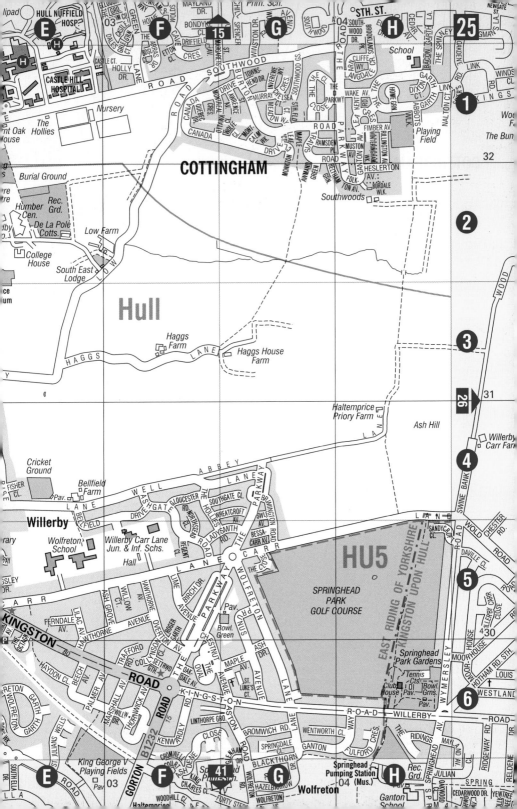

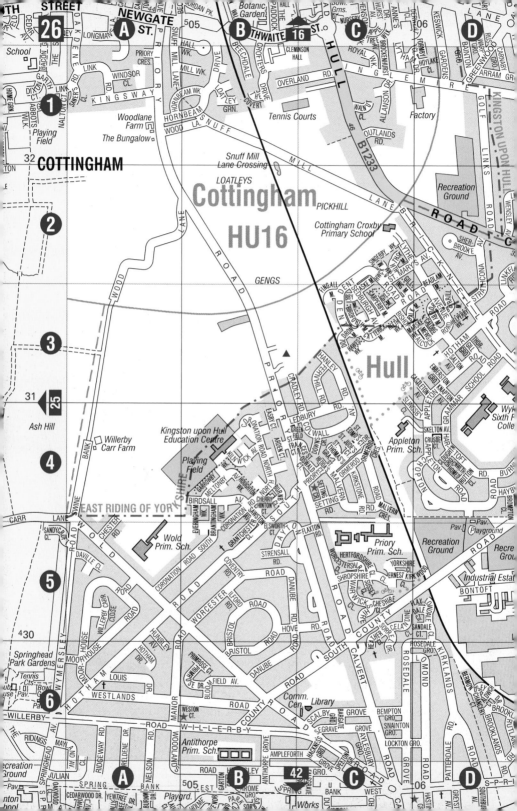

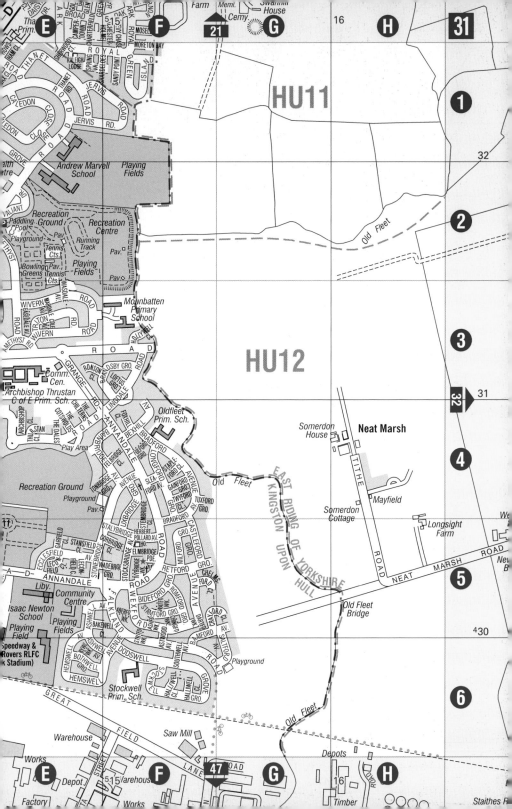

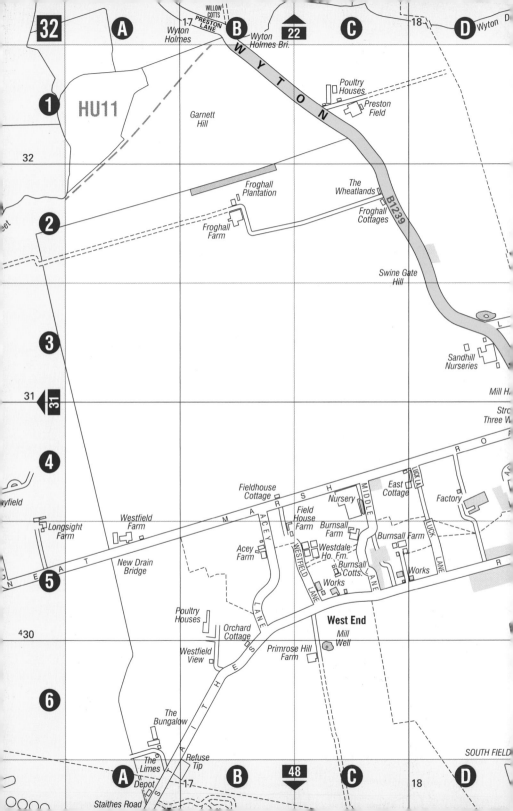

32 **A** **B** **C** **D**

WILLOW COTTS

1

HU11

Wyton Holmes

1·7

PRESTON LANE

Wyton Holmes Bri.

22

18

Wyton D

W Y T O N

Garnett Hill

Poultry Houses

Preston Field

32

Froghall Plantation

The Wheatlands

2

Froghall Farm

Froghall Cottages

B1239

Swine Gate Hill

3

Sandhill Nurseries

31

31

Mill H.

Str
Three W

4

Fieldhouse Cottage

M A R S H

Nursery

MIDDLE

East Cottage

Factory

LUCK LA.

ayfield

Longsight Farm

Westfield Farm

G A T E

Acey Farm

ACEY

Field House Farm

Burnsall Farm

WESTFIELD

Westdale Ho. Fm.

Burnsall Farm

LUCK LANE

Burnsall Cotts.

Works

R O

5

N

New Drain Bridge

LANE

Works

LANE

West End

Mill Well

R

30

Poultry Houses

Orchard Cottage

Westfield View

S

Primrose Hill Farm

6

The Bungalow

T A I T H E

A

The Limes

Refuse Tip

B

48

C

18

D

Depot

1·7

Staithes Road

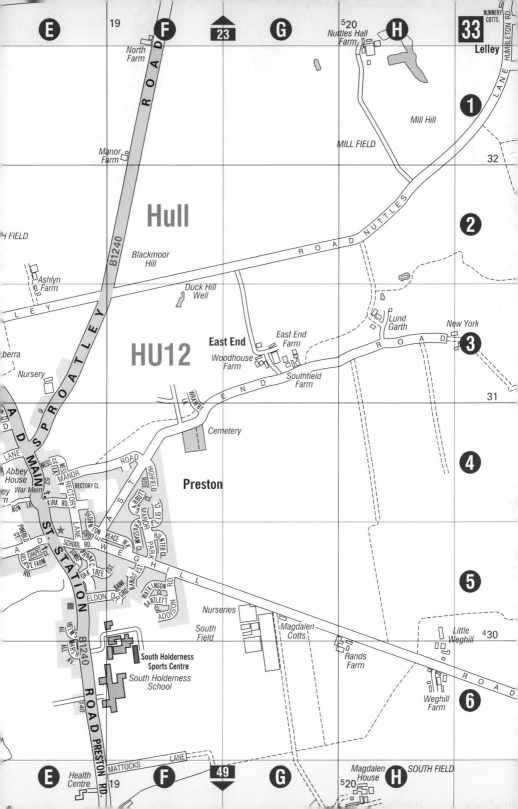

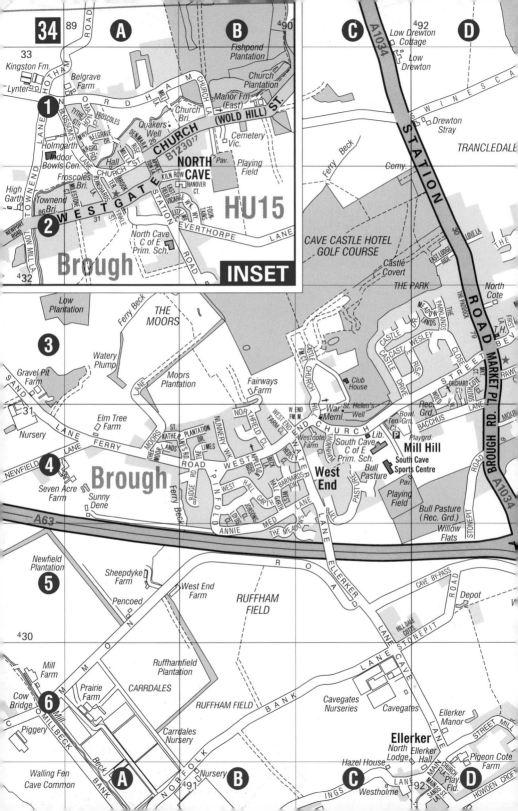

34 89

33

INSET

Brough

HU15

NORTH CAVE

Brough

West End

Mill Hill

Ellerker

RUFFHAM FIELD

CARRDALES

THE MOORS

CAVE CASTLE HOTEL GOLF COURSE

TRANCLEDALE

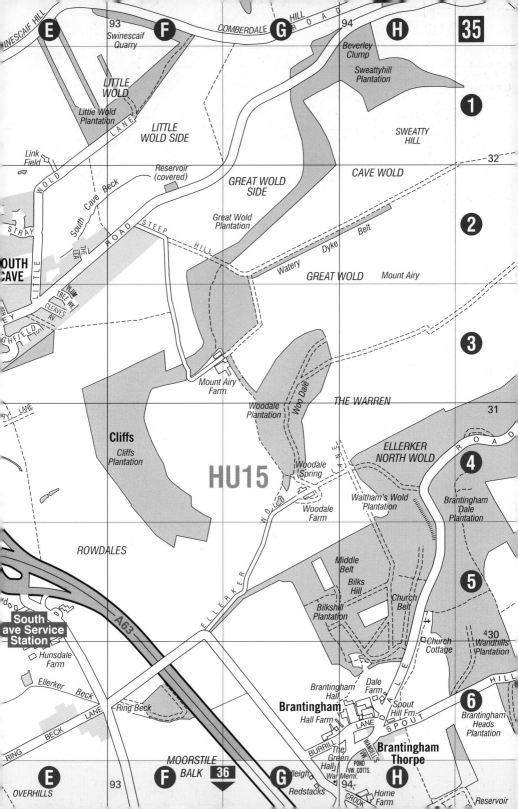

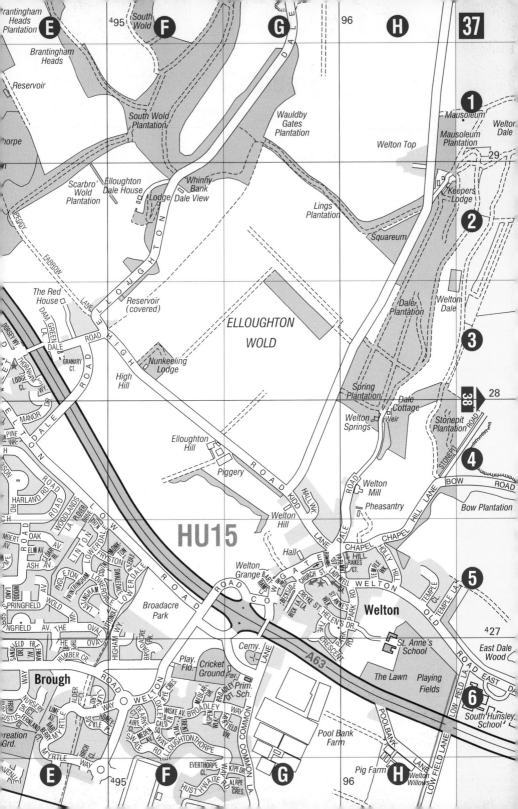

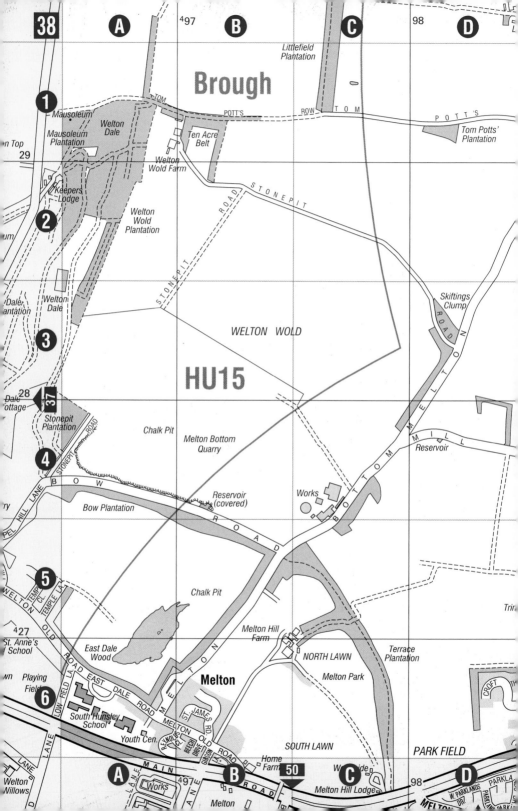

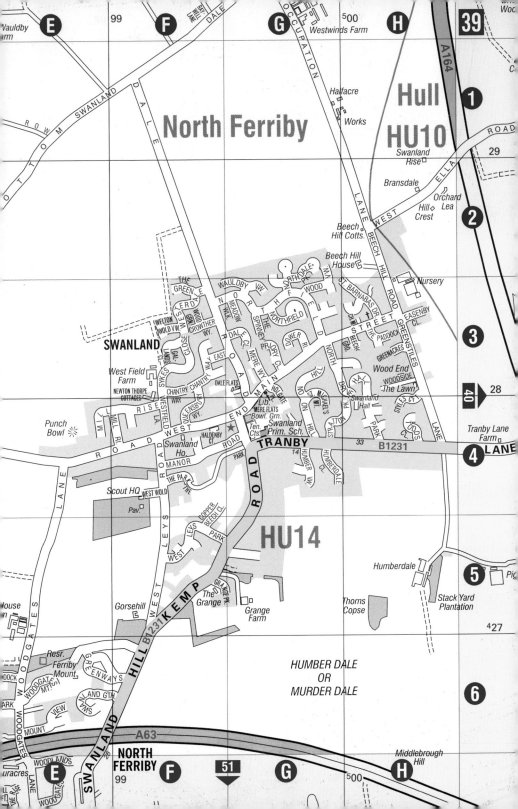

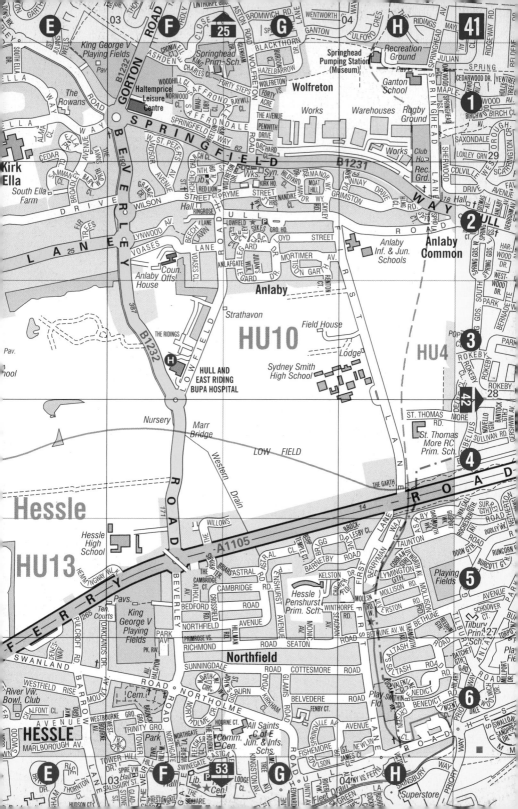

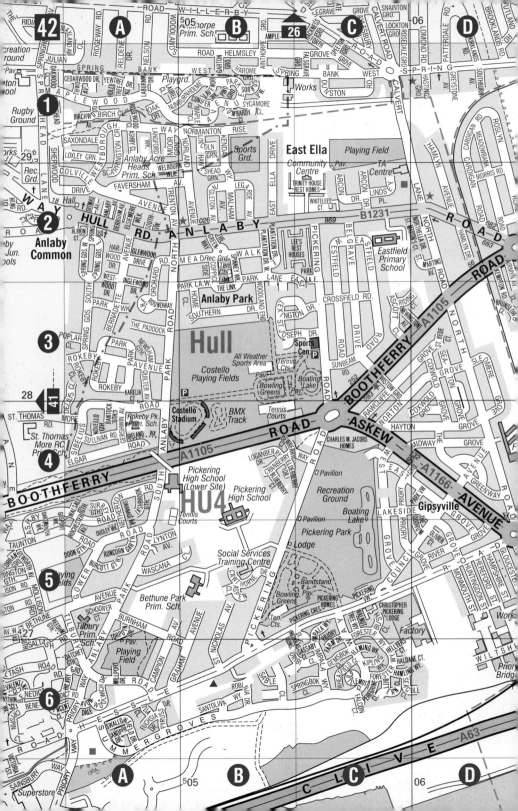

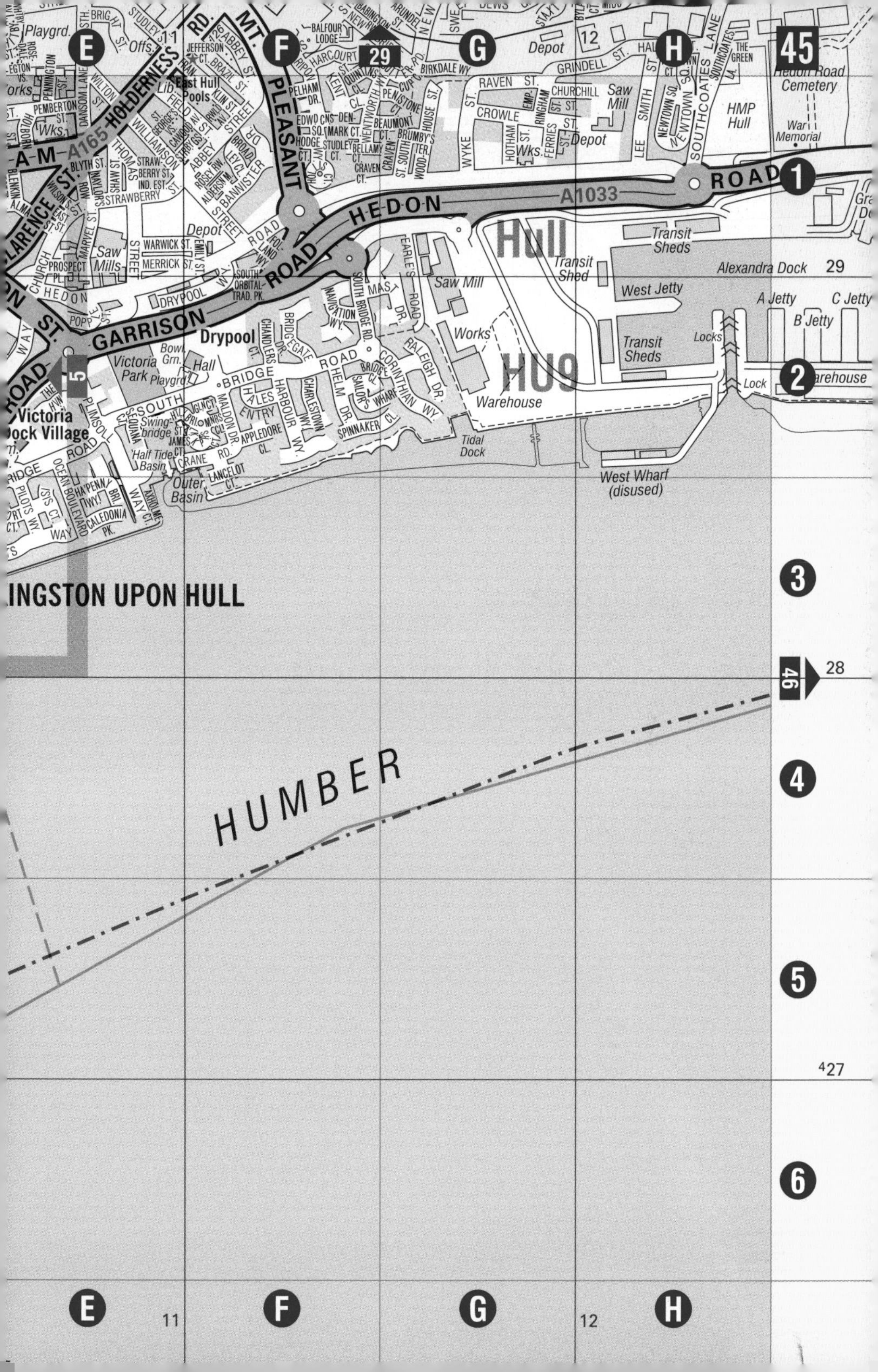

E
F
G
H
29
Hedon Road Cemetery
War Memorial
HMP Hull
HOLDERNESS RD.
A165
MT. PLEASANT
HEDON ROAD
A1033
ROAD
GARRISON ROAD
Hull
HU9
Drypool
Victoria Park
Victoria Dock Village
East Hull Pools
Alexandra Dock
West Jetty
Transit Sheds
Transit Shed
A Jetty
B Jetty
C Jetty
Locks
Lock
Warehouse
Saw Mill
Works
Tidal Dock
West Wharf (disused)
Outer Basin
Half Tide Basin
Swing-bridge
SOUTH BRIDGE ROAD
OCEAN BOULEVARD
CALEDONIA PK.
Depot
Wks.
GRINDELL ST.
RAVEN ST.
CHURCHILL ST.
CROWLE ST.
WYKE ST.
SOUTHCOATES LANE
NEWTOWN SQ.
KINGSTON UPON HULL
HUMBER
5
46
1
2
3
4
5
6
11
12
28
29
427

A **B** **C** **D**

HULL MATERNITY HOSPITAL

Hedon Road Cemetery

Works

HMP Hull

War Memorial

Works

30

Burial Ground

CARLTON AV.
FRODSHAM
DELHI
CYPRUS STREET
CLARENCE
CYPRUS ST
CEYLON

Depots

Port House

Depot

Warehouse

Depot

Pav. Works

Rec. Grd.

14

Marfleet

Works

Marfleet Prim. Sch.

Bowl. Grn.

ST NICHOLS AV
EDMONTON
FREDERICK
BROOKLYN
MARFLEET LANE

Works

Refinery

A1033

1

H E D O N

799

Graving Docks

Transit Sheds

29 Alexandra Dock

A Jetty

B Jetty

C Jetty

Transit Shed

Locks

Warehouse

2

Transit Shed

Customs and Excise House

Transit Sheds

CORPORATION ROAD

HOLDERNESS DRAIN

NORTHERN GATEWAY

Hull HU9

Riverside House

Transit Shed

Princess Margaret Passenger Terminal

Passenger Terminal Works

King Geor

Locks

Mas

P

River Terminal

Lock

3

4

28 **45**

R I V E R

Kingston upon Hull

North Lincolnshire

H U

5

4·27

6

A 13 **B** **C** 14 **D**

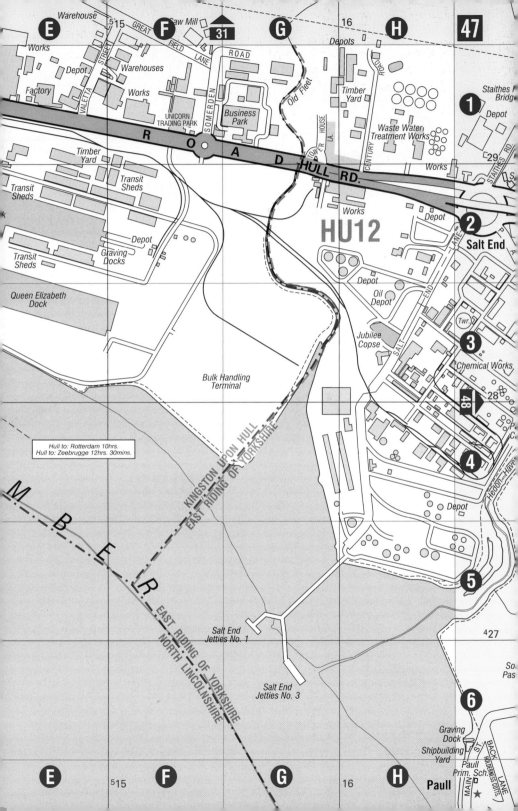

Warehouse
Works
Depot
Factory
Warehouses
Works
515 GREAT FIELD LANE
Saw Mill
31
SOMERDEN ROAD
Business Park
Unicorn Trading Park
VALETTA STREET

Depots
Timber Yard
Old Fleet
Waste Water Treatment Works
TOWER HOUSE LA.
CENTURY ROAD
Works
STAITHES RD.

Staithes Bridge
Depot
29

1

R O A D   HULL RD.

Timber Yard
Transit Sheds
Transit Sheds

Works
Depot
2 Salt End

Depot
Graving Docks
Transit Sheds
Depot

Queen Elizabeth Dock

HU12

Depot
Oil Depot
Jubilee Copse
SALT END LANE
Twr.
3
Chemical Works
28
48

4

Bulk Handling Terminal

Hull to: Rotterdam 10hrs.
Hull to: Zeebrugge 12hrs. 30mins.

KINGSTON UPON HULL
EAST RIDING OF YORKSHIRE

Depot

HEDON HAVEN

5

M B E R

EAST RIDING OF YORKSHIRE
NORTH LINCOLNSHIRE

Salt End Jetties No. 1

Salt End Jetties No. 3

4 27

So
Pas

6

Graving Dock
Shipbuilding Yard
Paull Prim. Sch.
MAIN ST.
BACK LANE
HOLDERNESS COTTS.

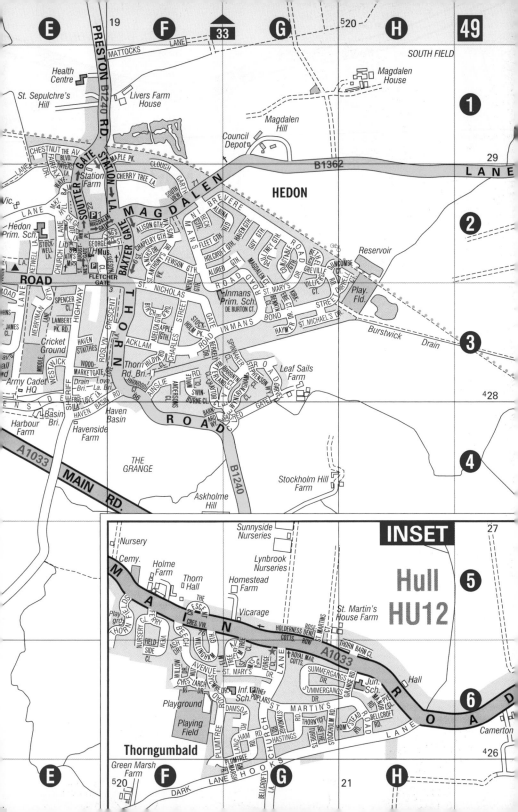

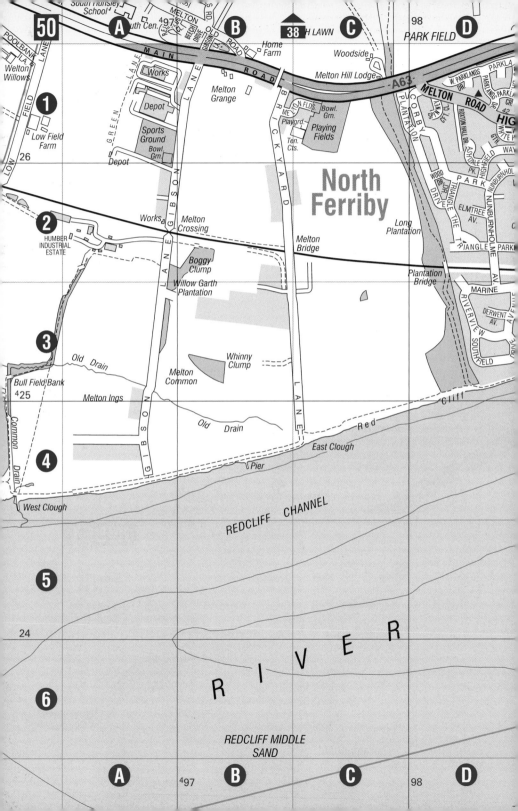

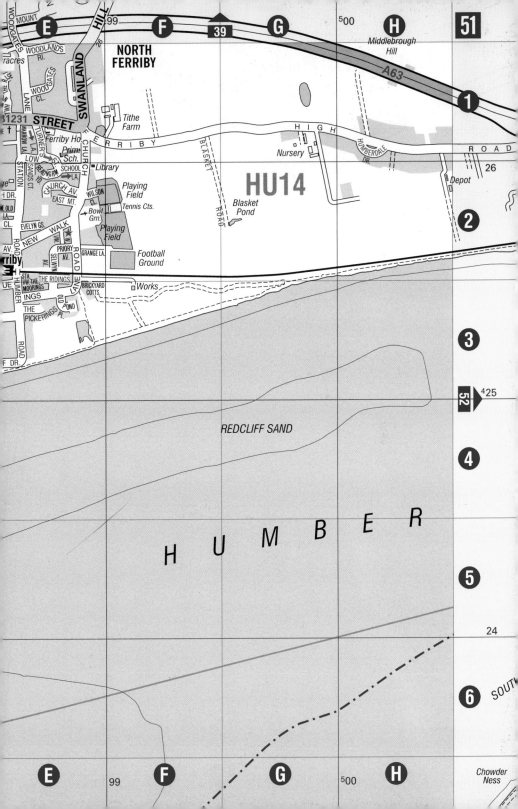

MOUNT
WOODGATES RI.
racres
WOODGATES CL.
SWANLAND HILL
26

NORTH FERRIBY

Tithe Farm

Middlebrough Hill

A63

1

HALL
STATION
B1231 **STREET**
†

Ferriby Ho.
Prim. Sch.
LOW READINGRM
SCHOOL LA.
CHURCH AV.
EAST MT.

NARROW LA.
TURNER'S LA.
SANDS CT.
CHURCH RD.

FERRIBY CHURCH RD.

Library

HIGH

Nursery

ROAD

HUMBERDALE DR.

26

Depot

HU14

BLASKET ROAD

Blasket Pond

2

Playing Field
Tennis Cts.
WILSON CL.
Bowl. Grn.
Playing Field
EVELYN GS.
NEW WALK
PRIORY AV.
GRANGE LA.
SELWYN WK.
ROAD LANE
ROAD
AV.

Football Ground

Ferriby
STA. VW.
MOORINGS
THE RIDINGS
HUMBER
INGS
THE PICKERINGS PL.
BRICKYARD COTTS.
OLD POND

Works

F DR.
ROAD
F DR.

3

REDCLIFF SAND

52 ▶ 425

4

H U M B E R

5

24

6 SOUT

Chowder Ness

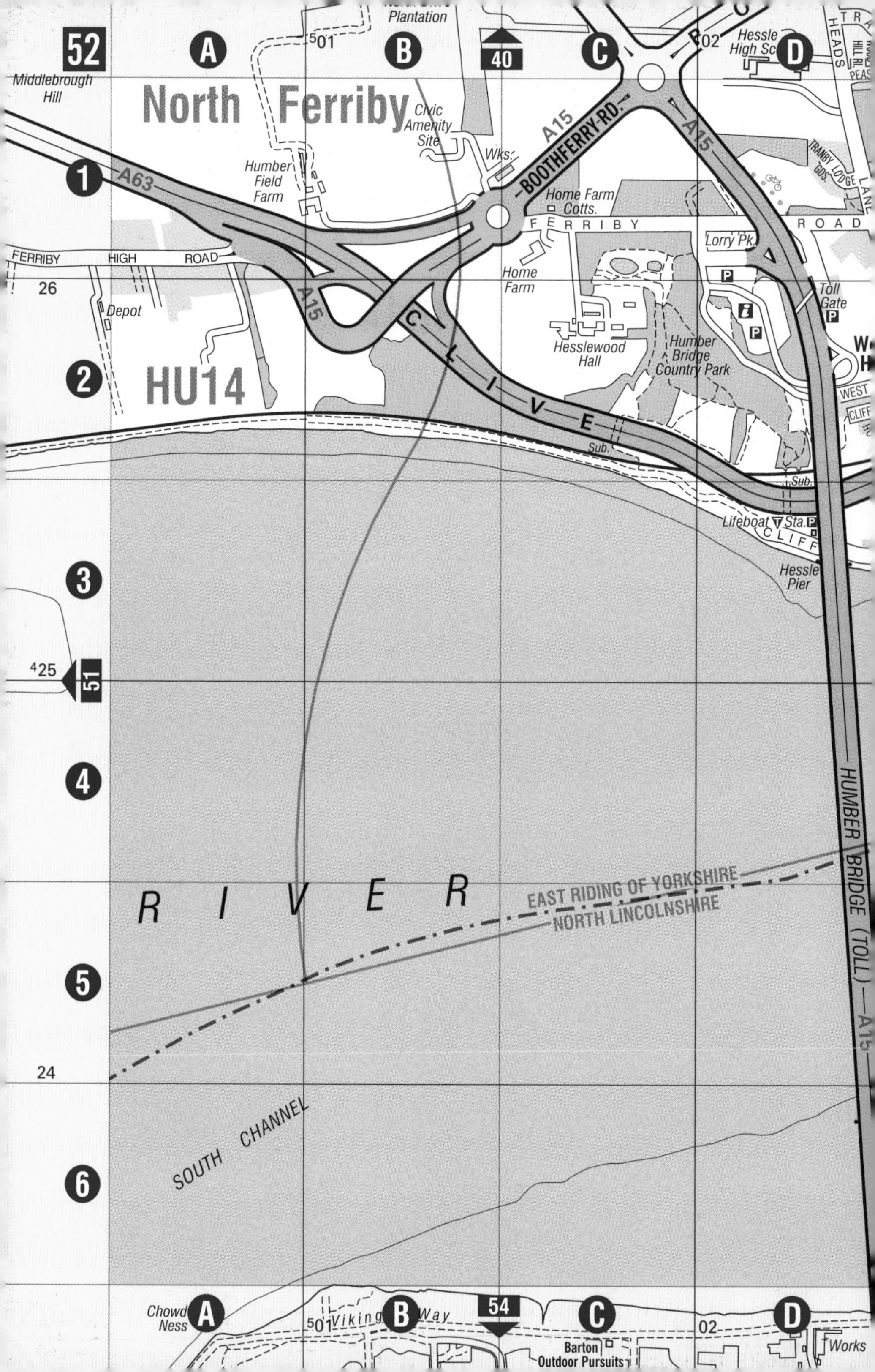

A   B   40   C   02   D

North Ferriby

Middlebrough Hill

Plantation

501

Hessle High Sc

Civic Amenity Site

Wks

1 A63   A15   BOOTHFERRY RD.   A15

Humber Field Farm

Home Farm Cotts.

Lorry Pk.

FERRIBY

Home Farm

FERRIBY HIGH ROAD

P

26

Depot

C

L

I

V

E

Hesslewood Hall

Humber Bridge Country Park

P

Toll Gate

i

P

2 HU14

ROAD

WEST

CLIFF

Sub.

Sub.

Lifeboat Sta. P

CLIFF

Hessle Pier

3

4 25 51

4

HUMBER BRIDGE (TOLL)   A15

R   I   V   E   R

EAST RIDING OF YORKSHIRE

NORTH LINCOLNSHIRE

5

24

SOUTH CHANNEL

6

Chowd Ness   A   501   Viking Way   B   54   C   02   D   Works

Barton Outdoor Pursuits

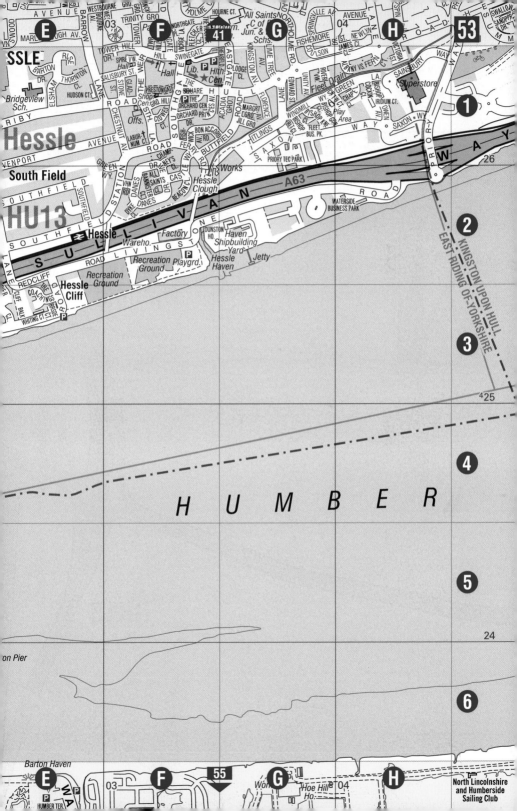

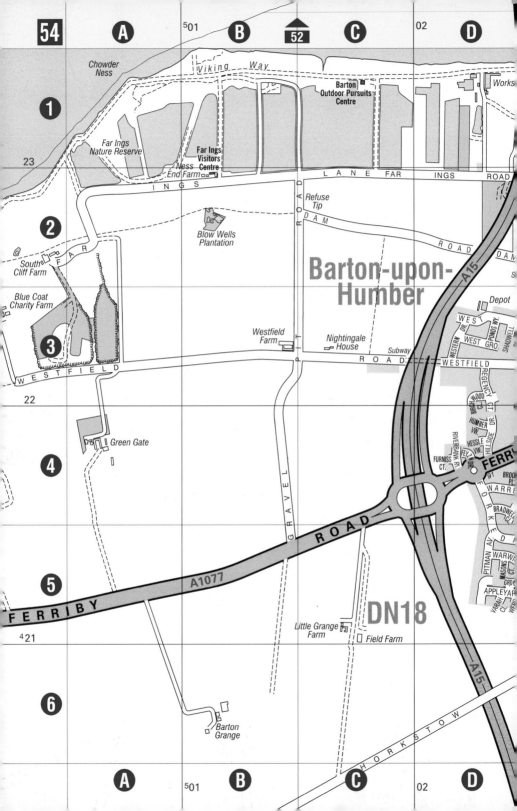

54

A ⁵01 B ▲52 C 02 D

1

Chowder Ness

Viking Way

Barton Outdoor Pursuits Centre

Works

23

Far Ings Nature Reserve

Far Ings Visitors Centre

Ness End Farm

I N G S   L A N E   F A R   I N G S   R O A D

2

Refuse Tip

R O A D

D A M

R O A D

D A M

Blow Wells Plantation

South Cliff Farm

F A R

Barton-upon-Humber

Depot

WEST DR.

WESTERN DR.

WEST GRO.

SPINUS WY.

SHADWELL

Blue Coat Charity Farm

3

Westfield Farm

Nightingale House

Subway

R O A D   WESTFIELD

REGENCY CT.

BIRCHWOOD CT.

W E S T F I E L D

22

HUMBER VW.

HESSLE VW.

HILLSIDE DR.

FURNISS CT.

RIVERBANK R.

FEY WK.

4

Green Gate

FERR

BROO PL.

WARRE

91

BRADWELL

GRAVEL

R O A D

PITMAN AV.

WARWI CT.

MASONS CT.

APPLEYAR

VARRH CL.

WEBS

5

A1077

DN18

Little Grange Farm

Field Farm

⁴21

F E R R I B Y

A15

6

Barton Grange

THORKSTOW

A ⁵01 B C 02 D

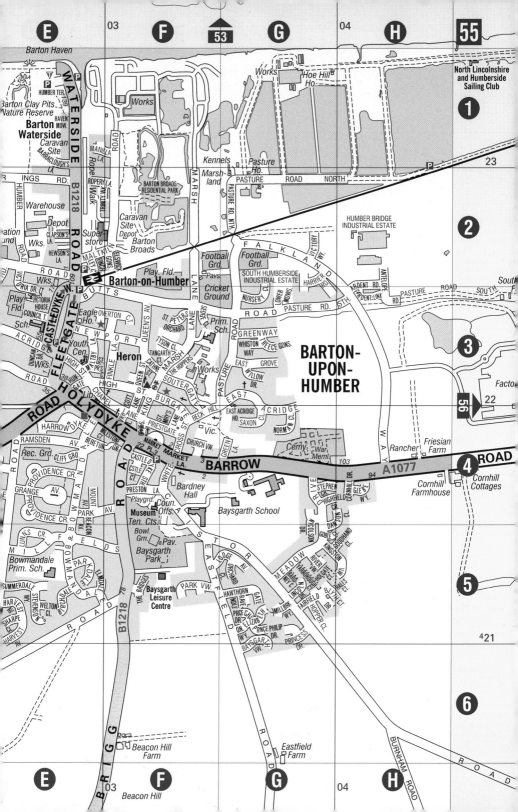

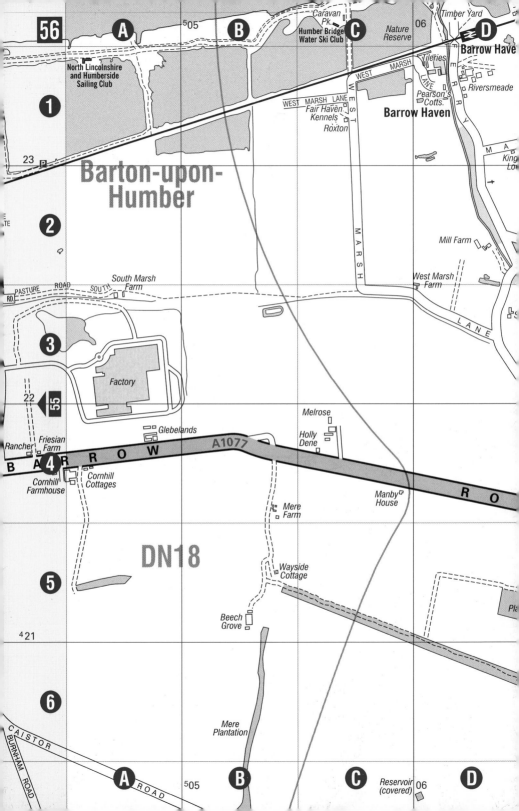

56

A ⁵05 B Caravan Pk. C 06 Timber Yard D

Humber Bridge
Water Ski Club

Nature
Reserve

Barrow Have

1

North Lincolnshire
and Humberside
Sailing Club

WEST   MARSH

Tileries

Pearson's
Cotts.

Riversmeade

WEST MARSH LANE

Fair Haven
Kennels

Roxton

WEST   MARSH

Barrow Haven

23

M A

King
Lo

Barton-upon-
Humber

2

MARSH

Mill Farm

TE

West Marsh
Farm

PASTURE   ROAD SOUTH

RD.

South Marsh
Farm

LANE

S

3

Factory

22 ◄ **55**

Melrose

4

Rancher

Friesian
Farm

Glebelands

A1077

Holly
Dene

B A R R O W

R O

Cornhill
Farmhouse

Cornhill
Cottages

Manby
House

DN18

Mere
Farm

5

Wayside
Cottage

⁴21

Beech
Grove

Pla

6

Mere
Plantation

CAISTOR

BURNHAM   ROAD

A R O A D ⁵05 B C 06 D

Reservoir
(covered)

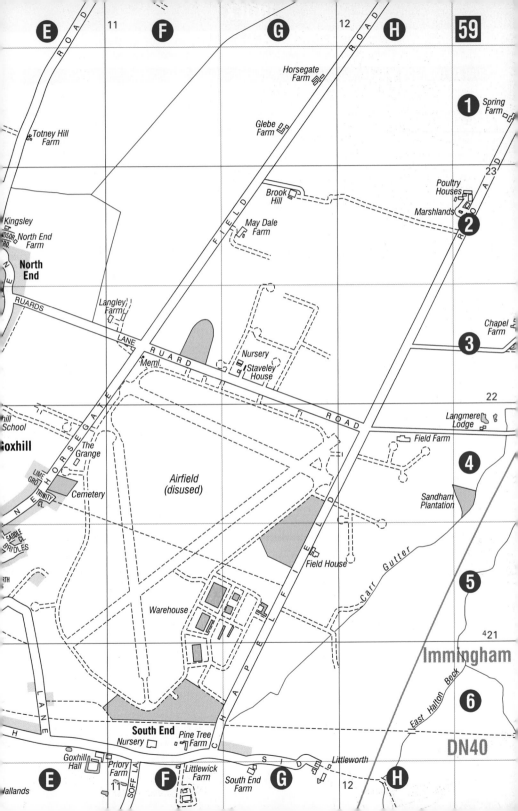

1 Spring Farm

Horsegate Farm

Glebe Farm

Totney Hill Farm

23

Poultry Houses
Marshlands

2

Brook Hill

Kingsley
North End Farm

May Dale Farm

North End

Chapel Farm

3

RUARDS

Langley Farm

LANE

RUARD ROAD

22

Meml.

Nursery
Staveley House

Langmere Lodge

hill School

Field Farm

Goxhill

The Grange

4

LIME GRO.
TRINITY CL.
SADDLE
BRIDLES

Cemetery

Airfield (disused)

Sandham Plantation

Field House

5

Carr Gutter

Warehouse

21

Immingham

South End

Pine Tree Farm

Nursery

DN40

6

East Halton Beck

Littleworth

Goxhill Hall

Priory Farm

Littlewick Farm

South End Farm

allands

INDEX

Including Streets, Places & Areas, Hospitals & Hospices, Industrial Estates,
Selected Flats & Walkways, Stations and Selected Places of Interest.

HOW TO USE THIS INDEX

1. Each street name is followed by its Postal District and then by its Locality abbreviation(s) and then by its map reference; e.g. **Abbey La.** HU10: Will . . . .4F **25** is in the Hull 10 Postal District and the Willerby Locality and is to be found in square 4F on page **25**. The page number is shown in bold type.

2. A strict alphabetical order is followed in which Av., Rd., St., etc. (though abbreviated) are read in full and as part of the street name; e.g. **Abbotsford Cl.** appears after **Abbots Cl.** but before **Abbots Wlk.**

3. Streets and a selection of flats and walkways too small to be shown on the maps, appear in the index with the thoroughfare to which it is connected shown in brackets; e.g. **Aigburth Av.** HU3: Hull. . . .3F **43** (off St George's Rd.)

4. Addresses that are in more than one part are referred to as not continuous.

5. Places and areas are shown in the index in **BLUE TYPE** and the map reference is to the actual map square in which the town centre or area is located and not to the place name shown on the map; e.g. **ANLABY.** 2G **41**

6. An example of a selected place of interest is **Barton Clay Pits Nature Reserve.** . . . 1E **55**

7. An example of a station is **Barrow Haven Station (Rail).** Included are Rail **(Rail)** and Park and Ride **(Park and Ride)**

8. An example of a hospital or hospice is **CASTLE HILL HOSPITAL.** . . .1E **25**

9. Map references shown in brackets; e.g. **Adelaide St.** HU1: Hull . . . .3B **44** (5B **4**) refer to entries that also appear on the large scale pages **4 & 5.**

GENERAL ABBREVIATIONS

All. : Alley	**Flds.** : Fields	**Nth.** : North
Arc. : Arcade	**Gdn.** : Garden	**Pde.** : Parade
Av. : Avenue	**Gdns.** : Gardens	**Pk.** : Park
Blvd. : Boulevard	**Gth.** : Garth	**Pl.** : Place
Bri. : Bridge	**Ga.** : Gate	**Ri.** : Rise
Bldgs. : Buildings	**Gt.** : Great	**Rd.** : Road
Bungs. : Bungalows	**Grn.** : Green	**Shop.** : Shopping
Bus. : Business	**Gro.** : Grove	**Sth.** : South
Cvn. : Caravan	**Hgts.** : Heights	**Sq.** : Square
Cen. : Centre	**Ho.** : House	**Sta.** : Station
Chu. : Church	**Ind.** : Industrial	**St.** : Street
Circ. : Circle	**Info.** : Information	**Ter.** : Terrace
Cl. : Close	**La.** : Lane	**Trad.** : Trading
Cotts. : Cottages	**Lit.** : Little	**Up.** : Upper
Ct. : Court	**Mans.** : Mansions	**Va.** : Vale
Cres. : Crescent	**Mkt.** : Market	**Vw.** : View
Cft. : Croft	**Mdw.** : Meadow	**Vs.** : Villas
Dr. : Drive	**Mdws.** : Meadows	**Wlk.** : Walk
E. : East	**M.** : Mews	**W.** : West
Ent. : Enterprise	**Mt.** : Mount	**Yd.** : Yard
Est. : Estate	**Mus.** : Museum	

LOCALITY ABBREVIATIONS

Anla : **Anlaby**	**Gox** : **Goxhill**	**Skid** : **Skidby**
Bar H : **Barrow-upon-Humber**	**Hed** : **Hedon**	**S'th C** : **South Cave**
Bart H : **Barton-upon-Humber**	**Hess** : **Hessle**	**Sproat** : **Sproatley**
Bev : **Beverley**	**Hull** : **Hull**	**Swan** : **Swanland**
Bil : **Bilton**	**King** : **Kingswood**	**Swin** : **Swine**
Brans : **Bransholme**	**Kir E** : **Kirk Ella**	**Thorn** : **Thorngumbald**
Brant : **Brantinghamthorpe**	**Mole** : **Molescroft**	**Tick** : **Tickton**
Brou : **Brough**	**New H** : **New Holland**	**Walk** : **Walkington**
Burt C : **Burton Constable**	**N'th C** : **North Cave**	**Waw** : **Wawne**
Coni : **Coniston**	**N'th F** : **North Ferriby**	**Welt** : **Welton**
Cott : **Cottingham**	**Paul** : **Paull**	**Will** : **Willerby**
Elle : **Ellerker**	**Prest** : **Preston**	**Wood** : **Woodmansey**
Ello : **Elloughton**	**Salt** : **Saltend**	

1st Av. HU6: Hull 6G 17
2nd Av. HU6: Hull 5G 17
4th Av. HU6: Hull 5G 17
5th Av. HU6: Hull 6E 17
6th Av. HU6: Hull 5F 17
7th Av. HU6: Hull 6G 17
8th Av. HU6: Hull 4F 17
9th Av. HU6: Hull 6G 17
10th Av. HU6: Hull .5G 17
11th Av. HU6: Hull .6G 17
12th Av. HU6: Hull .5F 17
14th Av. HU6: Hull .5F 17
15th Av. HU6: Hull .5F 17
16th Av. HU6: Hull .5F 17
17th Av. HU6: Hull .6F 17
18th Av. HU6: Hull .6F 17
19th Av. HU6: Hull .5F 17
20th Av. HU6: Hull .5F 17
21st Av. HU6: Hull .6F 17
22nd Av. HU6: Hull .5F 17
23rd Av. HU6: Hull .6F 17
24th Av. HU6: Hull .5F 17
25th Av. HU6: Hull .5F 17
26th Av. HU6: Hull .5E 17
27th Av. HU6: Hull .5E 17
28th Av. HU6: Hull .5E 17
29th Av. HU6: Hull .5F 17
30th Av. HU6: Hull (not continuous) 5E 17

31st Av. HU6: Hull .6E 17
32nd Av. HU6: Hull .5E 17
33rd Av. HU6: Hull .6E 17
34th Av. HU6: Hull .5E 17
36th Av. HU6: Hull .5E 17
37th Av. HU6: Hull .6D 16
38th Av. HU6: Hull .5E 17
40th Av. HU6: Hull .5E 17

A

Abbeygarth Vs. DN19: Gox 5E 59
Abbey La. HU10: Will. 4F 25
   HU12: Prest. 4D 32
Abbey Ri. DN19: Bar H 5G 57
Abbey Rd. HU11: Bil .5G 21
Abbey St. HU9: Hull. .6F 29
Abbots Cl. HU8: Hull .1H 29
Abbotsford Cl. HU5: Hull 4E 27
Abbots Wlk. HU16: Cott 1H 25
Aberdeen St. HU9: Hull 3A 30
Aberdovey Cl. HU7: Brans 5D 12
Aberford Wlk. HU9: Hull 5F 31
Abingdon Gth. HU7: Brans 2D 18
Acacia Dr. HU8: Hull .4G 29
Acacia Gro. HU13: Hess 1G 53
Acey La. HU12: Prest .5B 32
Acklam Rd. HU12: Hed 3F 49
Ackworth St. HU8: Hull 5F 29
Acland St. HU3: Hull .2F 43

Acorn Gro. HU8: Hull. 4H 19
Acorn Ind. Est. HU17: Bev 4H 7
Acorn Way HU13: Hess 5C 40
Acton Cl. HU8: Hull 1A 30
Ada Holmes Circ. HU6: Hull 5F 17
Adas Av. HU3: Hull 2G 43
Adderbury Cres. HU5: Hull 4A 28
Adderbury Gro. HU5: Hull 4A 28
Addison Gdns. HU8: Hull 3G 29
Addison Rd. HU12: Prest. 5F 33
Adelaide St. HU1: Hull 3B 44 (5B 4)
   HU3: Hull 3A 44 (5A 4)
Adeliza Gth. HU12: Hed 3F 49
Adelphi Cl. HU8: Hull .2A 30
Admirals Cft. HU1: Hull 3B 44 (6C 4)
Admiral Walker Rd. HU17: Bev 5D 6
Aigburth Av. HU3: Hull. 3F 43
   (off St George's Rd.)
Ainshaw HU6: Hull 4D 16
Ainslie Rd. HU12: Hed. 3F 49
Ainthorpe Gro. HU5: Hull 1B 42
Aintree Cl. HU17: Bev. 2D 6
Aire Cl. HU15: Brou 6F 37
Airedale HU7: Brans 6B 18
Airlie St. HU3: Hull 3G 43
Airmyn Av. HU3: Hull .2D 42
Air St. HU5: Hull 4C 28
Aisne St. HU5: Hull 6F 27
Ajax Cl. HU9: Hull 1E 31
Akester Cl. HU17: Bev. 5G 7
Alandale HU5: Hull (off Goddard Av.) 4G 27
Alandale Av. HU3: Hull 2E 43

Alaska Ct.—Barnard Way

Alaska Ct. HU8: Hull 5F **29**
Alaska St. HU8: Hull 5E **29**
Alaska Vs. *HU8: Hull (off Barnsley St.) 5E* ***29***
Albany St. HU3: Hull 6H **27**
Albany Vs. HU13: Hess 1H **53**
Albemarle Cl. HU15: Brou 6C **36**
Albermarle Rd. HU11: Bil 6H **21**
Albermarle St. HU3: Hull 3G **43**
Albert Av. *HU3: Hull (off Mayfield St.) 6H* ***27***
HU3: Hull (Spring Bank W.) 1E **43**
HU3: Hull (Wellsted St.) 3H **43**
HU3: Hull (off Rhodes St.) 3F ***43***
HU3: Hull (Boulevard) 4G **43**
HU9: Hull (off Middleburg St.) 6G ***29***
Albert Gro. HU3: Hull 4F **43**
Albert Sq. *HU5: Hull (off Ella St.) 4H* ***27***
Albert St. DN19: New H 2A **58**
Albert Ter. HU7: Hull 6G **19**
HU17: Bev 5D **6**
Albina Gth. HU12: Hed 2F **49**
Albion Av. HU3: Hull 2E **43**
Albion Ct. HU4: Anla 2A **42**
HU17: Bev 4G **7**
Albion Gro. HU3: Hull 3G **43**
Albion La. HU10: Will (not continuous) 3B **24**
Albion St. HU1: Hull 1B **44** (2C **4**)
Aldborough Gro. HU9: Hull 4B **30**
Aldbro' St. HU2: Hull 6C **28** (1E **5**)
Aldenham Pk. HU7: King 2A **18**
Alder Cl. HU15: Brou 6E **37**
Alder Hey Dr. HU8: Hull 1B **30**
Alderson M. HU9: Hull 1F **45**
Aldwych Ct. HU5: Hull 6D **26**
Alexandra Av. *HU3: Hull 6H* ***27***
(off Mayfield St.)
HU5: Hull 3H ***27***
(off Alexandra Rd.)
Alexandra Ct. HU5: Hull 3A **28**
Alexandra Dr. HU17: Bev 2D **8**
Alexandra Rd. HU5: Hull 3H **27**
Alexandra St. HU3: Hull 1A **44**
Alfonso St. HU3: Hull 3G **43**
Alfred Av. HU3: Hull 4F **43**
Alfred Gelder St. HU1: Hull 2C **44** (3D **4**)
Alfred St. HU3: Hull 3A **44** (6A **4**)
Alfriston Cl. HU7: Brans 6E **19**
Alison Gth. HU12: Hed 2F **49**
Allanhall Way HU10: Kir E 1C **40**
Allanson Dr. HU16: Cott 1C **26**
Allan Vale *HU9: Hull 6G* ***29***
(off Estcourt St.)
Allderidge Av. HU5: Hull 3F **27**
Allendale *HU9: Hull 6G* ***29***
(off Middleburg St.)
Allerford Dr. HU7: Brans 3D **18**
Allerthorpe Cres. HU15: Brou 6G **37**
All Hallows Rd. HU17: Walk 5B **8**
Alliance Av. HU3: Hull 1E **43**
Alliance La. HU3: Hull 1E **43**
Alloa Cl. HU6: Hull 4G **17**
All Saint's Cl. DN19: Gox 5D **58**
All Saints Cl. HU13: Hess 2F **53**
All Saints St. HU3: Hull 6A **28**
Alma Av. *HU5: Hull 4B* ***28***
(off Folkstone St.)
Alma Cl. HU10: Kir E 1E **41**
Alma St. HU9: Hull 1E **45** (2H **5**)
Almond Gro. HU3: Hull 2A **44** (4A **4**)
Alpha Av. HU17: Bev 2C **6**
Alston Av. HU8: Hull 5E **29**
Althorp Rd. HU7: King 3A **18**
Alured Gth. HU12: Hed 2F **49**
Alwoodley Cl. HU8: Hull 1C **30**
Amanda Cl. HU6: Hull 6E **17**
Amberley Cl. HU7: Brans 6D **18**
Amethyst Rd. HU9: Hull 2D **30**
AMF Bowling Kingston Upon Hull 6D **18**
Ampleforth Gro. HU5: Hull 6B **26**
Amsterdam Rd. HU7: Hull 1D **28**
Amy Johnson Ct. HU1: Hull 4C **4**
Amy's Gro. *HU3: Hull 3E* ***43***
(off Pretoria St.)
Ancaster Av. HU5: Hull 3D **26**
Anchor Ct. HU2: Hull 1C **4**
Anchor Rd. HU6: Hull 4H **17**
Ancourt HU6: Hull 6D **16**
Andersons Cl. HU12: Hed 3F **49**
Andrew La. HU12: Hed 3D **48**
Andrew Marvell Ho. HU1: Hull 4E **5**
ANLABY **2G 41**
Anlaby Av. HU4: Hull 2A **42**
ANLABY COMMON **2H 41**
ANLABY PARK **2B 42**
Anlaby Pk. Rd. Nth. HU4: Hull 4A **42**
Anlaby Pk. Rd. Sth. HU4: Hull 6A **42**
Anlaby Rd. HU1: Hull 2A **44** (4A **4**)
HU3: Hull 2B **42** (4A **4**)
HU4: Hull 2B **42**
Anlafgate HU10: Anla 2G **41**
Annandale Rd. HU9: Hull 4F **31**
HU10: Kir E 5C **24**
Anne St. HU1: Hull 2B **44** (4C **4**)
Annie Med La. HU15: S'th C 5B **34**
Annie Reed Ct. HU17: Bev 5H **7**
Annie Reed Rd. HU17: Bev 5H **7**
Ann Watson St. HU7: Hull 2D **28**
Anson Rd. HU9: Hull 3C **30**
Antelope Rd. DN18: Bart H 2H **55**
Antholme Cl. HU7: Hull 6F **19**
Antwerp Rd. HU7: Hull 1D **28**
Apollo Wlk. HU8: Hull 2A **30**
Appin Cl. HU7: Brans 6D **12**
Apple Cft. HU16: Skid 4C **14**
Appledore Cl. HU9: Hull 2F **45**
Apple Gth. HU12: Hed 3F **49**
Applegarth M. HU16: Cott 5H **15**
Applegarth Rd. HU8: Hull 1D **44** (1G **5**)
Appleton Gdns. HU15: S'th C 4B **34**
Appleton La. HU15: N'th C 1A **34**
Appleton Rd. HU5: Hull 4D **26**
Apple Tree Cl. HU8: Hull 2G **29**
Apple Tree Wlk. HU16: Cott 6C **16**
Appleyard Dr. DN18: Bart H 5D **54**
Archbishop Cl. HU9: Hull 4E **31**
Arcon Dr. HU4: Hull 2C **42**
Arctic Corsair **2D 44** (**3G 5**)
Arden Ct. HU5: Hull 4B **26**
Arden Rd. HU17: Bev 3F **7**
Ardent Link DN18: Bart H 3H **55**
Ardent Rd. DN18: Bart H 3H **55**
Ardmore Cl. HU9: Hull 2C **30**
Argent Cl. HU6: Hull 4G **17**
Argyle Av. *HU9: Hull 6G* ***29***
(off Middleburg St.)
Argyle St. HU3: Hull 1H **43**
Arkley Cl. HU15: Brou 6D **36**
Ark Royal HU11: Bil 6E **21**
Arlington Av. *HU5: Hull (off Perth St.) 6F* ***27***
HU16: Cott 6A **16**
Arlington St. HU3: Hull 2A **44**
Armstrong Cl. HU17: Bev 5F **7**
Arncliffe Cl. HU7: Brans 6C **12**
Arncliffe Way HU16: Cott 1H **25**
Arnold La. HU3: Hull 2G **43**
Arnold St. HU3: Hull 2H **43**
Arram Gro. HU6: Hull 1D **26**
Arran Cl. HU9: Hull 2B **30**
Arras Dr. HU16: Cott 1F **25**
Arreton Cl. HU8: Hull 6E **21**
Arthur Lucan Ct. HU9: Hull 5D **30**
Arthur St. HU3: Hull 3F **43**
Arundel Ct. HU9: Hull 6F **29**
Arundel St. HU9: Hull 6G **29**
Ascott Cl. HU4: Hull 3C **42**
HU17: Bev 1D **6**
Asenby Wlk. *HU5: Hull (off Dent Rd.) 3C* ***26***
Ash Av. HU15: Ello 5E **37**
Ashbourne Gro. *HU3: Hull (off Greek St.) 3F* ***43***
Ashbrook *HU8: Hull 5E* ***29***
(off Buckingham St.)
Ashbury Ct. HU6: Hull 6F **17**
Ashby Cl. HU4: Hull 1A **42**
Ashby Rd. HU4: Hull 5H **41**
Ash Cl. HU11: Sproat 3F **23**
HU13: Hess 5D **40**
HU17: Bev 2E **7**
Ashcombe Rd. HU7: King 3A **18**
Ashdale Lodge HU3: Hull 2E **43**
Ashdale Pk. HU14: N'th F 1D **50**
Ashdene *HU5: Hull (off Goddard Av.) 4H* ***27***
HU17: Walk 2C **8**
Ash Dene Cl. HU10: Will 1F **41**
Ashdene Vs. *HU8: Hull (off Brecon St.) 5E* ***29***
Ash Dr. HU10: Will 6G **25**
HU12: Thorn 6F **49**
Ashendon Dr. HU8: Hull 4D **28**
Ashford Wlk. HU9: Hull 5F **31**
Ashgate Rd. HU10: Will 4F **25**
Ash Gro. *HU3: Hull (off Greek St.) 3E* ***43***
HU3: Hull (off De La Pole Av.) 1E ***43***
HU5: Hull (Perth St.) 6G **27**
HU5: Hull (Beverley Rd.) 3H **27**
HU10: Will 5F **25**
Ashington Wlk. HU8: Hull 5D **20**
Ashmole Wlk. HU17: Bev 3F **7**
Ashthorpe HU6: Hull 4E **17**
Ashton Cl. HU6: Hull 4E **17**
Ashwell Av. HU9: Hull 5E **31**
Ashworth Dr. HU10: Kir E 5C **24**
Ashworthy Cl. HU7: Brans 3B **18**
Aske M. HU5: Hull 3C **26**
Askew Av. HU4: Hull 4C **42**
Askrigg Wlk. *HU5: Hull 3C* ***26***
(off Dent Rd.)
Aspall Wlk. HU8: Hull 5D **20**
Aspen Cl. HU4: Hull 5B **42**
Aspen Wlk. HU15: Brou 6F **37**
Assaby Cl. HU4: Hull 6C **42**
Astley St. HU3: Hull 1E **43**
Aston Hall Dr. HU14: N'th F 1E **51**
Aston Rd. HU10: Will 6G **25**
Astoria Cres. HU8: Hull 2A **30**
Astral Cl. HU7: Brans 5G **19**
HU13: Hess 5G **41**
Astral Gdns. HU7: Brans 5F **19**
Astral Rd. HU13: Hess 5G **41**
Astral Way HU7: Brans 5G **19**
Astwood Av. HU9: Hull 5F **31**
Athelstan Rd. HU17: Bev 3E **7**
Athens Cl. HU3: Hull 3E **43**
Athletic Gro. HU3: Hull 3G **43**
Athlone Grn. HU8: Hull 1D **30**
Atholl Av. HU13: Hess 5F **41**
Athol St. HU3: Hull 3E **43**
Atkinson Dr. HU15: Brou 5D **36**
Atlanta Ct. HU8: Hull 1C **30**
Atwick Ct. HU9: Hull 5C **30**
Auburn Cl. HU9: Hull 5D **30**
Auckland Av. HU6: Hull 2H **27**
Auckland Ho. HU1: Hull 3B **44** (5B **4**)
Audley St. HU2: Hull 6B **28**
Augusta Cl. HU8: Hull 6C **20**
Augustine's Ct. HU5: Hull 3A **28**
Augustus Dr. HU15: Brou 6E **37**
Autherd Gth. HU17: Walk 6C **8**
Avenue Cres., The *HU3: Hull 3G* ***43***
(off Albermarle St.)
Avenue Halcyon HU13: Hess 6F **41**
Avenues Ct. HU5: Hull 5H **27**
Avenue, The HU3: Hull 3F **43**
HU4: Hull 5D ***42***
(off Hampshire St.)
HU7: Hull 6H **19**
HU10: Anla 1G **41**
HU10: Kir E 1D **40**
HU16: Cott 6H ***15***
(off Crescent St.)
Avondale HU4: Hull 6A **42**
HU5: Hull 4H ***27***
(off Goddard Av.)
HU9: Hull 5G ***29***
(off Rustenburg St.)
Avondale Cres. *HU5: Hull 6F* ***27***
(off Perth St. W.)
Avon St. HU8: Hull 5F **29**
Avon Vale *HU9: Hull 6H* ***29***
(off Estcourt St.)
Awmand Grn. HU16: Cott 2G **25**
Axdane HU6: Hull 5D **16**
Axholme Ct. HU9: Hull 3E **45**
Axminster Cl. HU7: Brans 4D **18**
Aylesbury Gro. HU5: Hull 6C **26**
Aylesford St. HU3: Hull 3G **43**
Aysgarth Av. HU6: Hull 2D **26**

B

Babington Row HU9: Hull 6F **29**
Bacchus La. HU15: S'th C 4D **34**
Bacheler St. HU3: Hull 3G **43**
Back La. HU12: Paul 6A **48**
Back Rd. HU11: Burt C 1F **23**
Bacon Gth. La. HU16: Cott 1H **25**
(not continuous)
Baden Cl. HU5: Hull 4A **28**
Badgers Wood HU16: Cott 4G **15**
Bagby M. HU5: Hull 3C **26**
Bailey La. HU16: Cott 4C **16**
Bainbridge Av. HU9: Hull 4E **31**
Bainton Cl. HU17: Bev 3C **6**
Bainton Gro. HU6: Hull 6D **16**
Baker St. HU2: Hull 1B **44** (2C **4**)
Bakewell Cl. HU9: Hull 5E **31**
Balfour Lodge HU9: Hull 6F **29**
Balfour St. HU9: Hull 6F **29**
Balham Av. HU8: Hull 6H **19**
Balk La. HU11: Sproat 3F **23**
Balk M. HU5: Hull 3C **26**
Ballantyne Cl. HU7: Hull 2F **29**
Ballathie Cl. HU6: Hull 3G **17**
Balmoral Av. HU6: Hull 6G **17**
Balmoral Dr. HU17: Bev 1F **9**
Bamford Av. HU9: Hull 5F **31**
Bankside HU5: Hull 4C **28**
Bankside Ind. Est. HU5: Hull 3C **28**
Bannister Cl. HU13: Hess 2F **53**
Bannister Dr. HU9: Hull 1F **45**
Bantock Gth. HU4: Anla 4A **42**
Barbarry Rd. HU12: Hed 2D **48**
Barberry Ct. HU3: Hull 3H **43**
HU15: Brou 6E **37**
Bardney Cl. DN18: Bart H 5G **55**
Bardshaw HU6: Hull 4E **17**
Bargate Gro. HU5: Hull 6C **26**
Barham Rd. HU9: Hull 3D **30**
Barkers Mill HU17: Bev 5G **7**
Barking Cl. HU8: Hull 1B **30**
Barkworth Cl. HU10: Anla 2E **41**
Barleigh Cft. HU9: Hull 3C **30**
Barleigh Rd. HU9: Hull 3B **30**
Barmouth Ct. HU7: Brans 5D **12**
Barmston Cl. HU17: Bev 3G **7**
Barmston La. HU17: Wood 3D **10**
Barmston Rd. HU17: Bev 3G **7**
Barmston St. HU2: Hull 6C **28**
Barnards Dr. HU15: S'th C 4B **34**
Barnard Way HU12: Hed 4F **49**

A-Z Hull 61

Barnes Cl.—Brandsby Gro.

Barnes Cl. HU17: Bev 4G **7**
Barnetby Rd. HU13: Hess 5G **41**
Barnet Cl. HU8: Hull 1B **30**
Barnsley Bldgs. HU8: Hull 5F **29**
Barnsley St. HU8: Hull 5E **29**
Barnstaple Rd. HU7: Brans 5E **19**
Baroness Cl. HU6: Hull 4G **17**
Barra Cl. HU8: Hull 6A **20**
Barraclough's La. DN18: Bart H 1E **55**
Barrick Cl. DN19: Bar H 5F **57**
Barrington Av. HU5: Hull 3E **27**
Barrow Ct. HU3: Hull 5A **28**
BARROW HANN **3G 57**
BARROW HAVEN **1D 56**
Barrow Haven Station (Rail) **1D 56**
Barrow Lane HU13: Hess 6E **41**
Barrow Rd. DN18: Bar H, Bart H 4G **55**
DN19: Bar H 4G **55**
DN19: New H 2A **58**
BARROW-UPON-HUMBER **5F 57**
Bartlett Av. HU17: Bev 5D **6**
Bartlett Cl. HU12: Prest 5F **33**
Barton Broads Residential Pk. DN18: Bart H 2F **55**
Barton Clay Pits Nature Reserve 1E 55
Barton Dr. HU13: Hess 1E **53**
Barton La. DN19: Bar H 5E **57**
Barton-on-Humber Station (Rail) **2E 55**
Barton Outdoor Pursuits Cen. 1C 54
Barton St. DN19: Bar H 4F **57**
BARTON-UPON-HUMBER **3F 55**
BARTON WATERSIDE **1E 55**
Bartrams HU15: Welt 5G **37**
Basil Dr. HU17: Bev 6D **6**
Bathurst St. HU3: Hull 3A **44** (6A **4**)
Batley Cl. HU9: Hull 4D **30**
Battersea Cl. HU8: Hull 1A **30**
Baxter Ga. HU12: Hed 2F **49**
Bay Ct. HU17: Bev 2E **9**
Baynard Av. HU16: Cott 6H **15**
Baysdale HU7: Brans 6C **18**
Baysgarth House Mus. 4F 55
Baysgarth Leisure Cen. 5F 55
Baysgarth Vw. DN18: Bart H 5G **55**
Bayswater Ct. HU8: Hull 1A **30**
Beacon Av. DN18: Bart H 4E **55**
Beacon Cl. HU13: Hess 2F **53**
Beaconsfield Gdns. *HU5: Hull* *3H 27*
(off Raglan St.)
Beaconsfield St. HU5: Hull 4A **28**
Beaconsfield Vs. *HU9: Hull* *6F 29*
(off Holland St.)
Beadlam M. HU5: Hull 2D **26**
Beamsley Way HU7: King 1B **18**
Bearwood Cl. HU8: Hull 6C **20**
Beaufort Cl. HU3: Hull 3A **44**
Beaulieu Ct. HU9: Hull 3B **30**
Beaumont Ct. HU9: Hull 1G **45**
Beautiman Ct. HU6: Hull 6F **17**
Beaver Rd. HU17: Bev 4G **7**
Beccles Cl. HU8: Hull 6C **20**
Beck Bank HU16: Cott 6A **16**
Beckdale HU7: Brans 6D **18**
Beck Gth. HU12: Hed 2F **49**
Beck Hill DN18: Bart H 4F **55**
Beckhole Cl. HU3: Hull 2F **43**
Beckington Cl. HU8: Hull 5D **20**
Beck La. DN19: Bar H 4F **57**
HU15: S'th C 4B **34**
HU15: Welt 5G **37**
Beckside HU15: Welt 5G **37**
HU17: Bev 5F **7**
Beckside Cl. HU6: Hull 5G **17**
Beckside Nth. HU17: Bev 5G **7**
Beck Vw. Rd. HU17: Bev 5H **7**
Bedale Av. HU9: Hull 5H **29**
Bedford Rd. HU13: Hess 5F **41**
Bedford St. HU8: Hull 5D **28**
Bedford St. Cvn. Site HU8: Hull 5D **28**
Beech Av. HU8: Hull 4F **29**
HU10: Will 6E **25**
HU11: Bil 6G **21**
HU12: Hed 2D **48**
HU12: Thorn 5F **49**
HU17: Bev 2E **7**
Beechcliffe Av. HU6: Hull 5H **17**
Beech Cl. HU3: Hull 3H **43**
HU11: Sproat 2E **23**
Beechdale HU16: Cott 6B **16**
Beech Dr. HU14: N'th F 2E **51**
HU14: Welt 6B **38**
Beeches, The *HU5: Hull* *3H 27*
(off Sidmouth St.)
HU5: Hull *4H 27*
(off Goddard Av.)
Beechfield HU6: Hull 6G **17**
Beechfield Dr. HU10: Will 4D **24**
Beech Gth. DN19: Bar H 6E **57**
Beech Gro. HU3: Hull 3E **43**
(Ringrose St.)
HU3: Hull 3H **43**
(Wellsted St.)
HU5: Hull *6G 27*
(off Perth St.)
Beech Gro. HU5: Hull (Strath St.) 3H **27**
HU5: Hull (off Reynoldson St.) *4H 27*
HU5: Hull (Prince's Rd.) 4H **27**
HU8: Hull (off Lorraine St.) *3D 28*
HU13: Hess 5D **40**
HU14: Swan 3H **39**
Beech Hill Rd. HU14: Swan 2H **39**
Beech Holme Ct. HU5: Hull 3A **28**
Beech Lawn HU10: Anla 2F **41**
Beech Rd. HU15: Ello 4D **36**
Beech Tree Cl. HU17: Bev 1E **7**
Beech Vw. HU17: Walk 5C **8**
Beechwood Ct. HU9: Hull 5G **29**
Beeford Gro. HU6: Hull 1E **27**
Beilby St. HU3: Hull 3E **43**
Belfry Ct. HU8: Hull 6C **20**
Belgrave Dr. HU4: Hull 2C **42**
HU15: N'th C 1A **34**
Bellamy Ct. HU9: Hull 1F **45**
Bell Cl. HU7: Hull 6G **19**
Bellcroft La. HU12: Thorn 6G **49**
Bellcroft Rd. HU12: Thorn 6H **49**
Belle-Vue *HU9: Hull* *6G 29*
(off Middleburg St.)
Bellfield Av. HU8: Hull 6H **19**
Bellfield Dr. HU10: Will 4E **25**
Bells Rd. HU12: Hed 3D **48**
Belmont Farm *HU13: Hess (off Cliff Rd.)* *3E 53*
Belmont St. HU9: Hull 6G **29**
Belphrin Rd. HU17: Bev 3G **7**
Beltham Grn. HU16: Cott 2G **25**
Belton Cl. HU8: Hull 1C **30**
Belvedere Dr. HU11: Bil 6E **21**
Belvedere Rd. HU13: Hess 6G **41**
Belvoir St. HU5: Hull 6G **27**
Bempton Gro. HU5: Hull 6C **26**
Benedict Rd. HU4: Hull 6H **41**
Bennington Cl. HU12: Hed 3G **49**
BENTLEY **6D 8**
Bentley Ct. HU3: Hull 3F **43**
Bentley Gro. HU6: Hull 2E **27**
Berberis Cl. HU3: Hull 3H **43**
Beresford Av. HU6: Hull 2A **28**
HU9: Hull (off Middleburg St.) *6G 29*
Beretun Grn. DN18: Bart H 4E **55**
Bergen Way HU7: Hull 6A **18**
Berkeley Dr. HU17: Bev 1F **9**
Berkeley St. HU3: Hull 5A **28**
Berkely Dr. HU12: Hed 3F **49**
Berkshire Cl. HU17: Bev 2F **9**
Berkshire St. HU8: Hull 5F **29**
Bermondsey Dr. HU5: Hull 6D **26**
Bernadette Av. HU4: Anla 3A **42**
Berryman Way HU13: Hess 5H **41**
Bessacarr Av. HU10: Will 5G **25**
Bessingby Gro. HU9: Hull 4C **30**
Beta Vs. *HU3: Hull (off Mayfield St.)* *6H 27*
Bethel Cl. HU12: Hed 2G **49**
Bethune Av. HU4: Hull 5H **41**
Bethune Av. W. HU4: Hull 5H **41**
Betula Ct. HU8: Hull 5H **19**
BEVERLEY **4F 7**
Beverley Dr. HU17: Bev 1C **6**
Beverley Leisure Cen. 5F 7
Beverley Minster 5E 7
Beverley Parklands HU17: Bev 6F **7**
Beverley Race Course 4A 6
Beverley Rd. HU3: Hull 3A **28** (1B **4**)
HU5: Hull 3A **28**
HU6: Hull, Wood (not continuous) 6F **11**
HU10: Anla, Hess, Kir E, Will 4C **24**
HU13: Hess 1F **41**
HU15: S'th C 3D **34**
HU16: Skid 3D **14**
Beverley Road Baths 5A 28
Beverley Station (Rail) **4E 7**
Beverley Swimming Pool 4E 7
Bewick Gro. HU9: Hull 4A **30**
Bexhill Av. HU9: Hull 4F **31**
Bibury Cl. HU8: Hull 4E **29**
Bickerton Cl. HU6: Hull 5E **17**
Bickleigh Gro. HU8: Hull 6D **20**
Bideford Gro. HU9: Hull 5F **31**
Bielby Dr. HU17: Bev 5G **7**
Biggin Av. HU7: Brans 4E **19**
Bilsdale Gro. HU9: Hull 6A **30**
BILTON **5H 21**
Bilton Gro. HU9: Hull 5C **30**
Binbrook Gth. HU7: Brans 2E **19**
Binfield Sq. *HU5: Hull (off Ella St.)* *4H 27*
Birch Cl. HU5: Hull 1A **42**
HU13: Hess 5C **40**
HU15: Brou 6E **37**
HU17: Bev 2E **7**
Birch Cft. HU15: Ello 5D **36**
Birchdale DN18: Bart H 5E **55**
Birch Dr. HU10: Will 5F **25**
Birch Lea HU17: Walk 5A **8**
Birch Leigh HU3: Hull 2H **43**
Birchwood Av. HU5: Hull 1A **42**
Birchwood Cl. DN18: Bart H 3D **54**
Birdforth M. HU5: Hull 3C **26**
Birdsall Av. HU5: Hull 4B **26**
Birdsall Cl. HU16: Cott 1F **25**
Birkby Gro. HU9: Hull 4D **30**
Birkdale Cl. HU10: Kir E 6C **24**
Birkdale Way HU9: Hull 6G **29**
Birklands Dr. HU8: Hull 2H **29**
Bishop Alcock Rd. HU5: Hull 3C **26**
Bishop Blunt Cl. HU13: Hess 1G **53**
Bishop Cockin Cl. HU13: Hess 1H **53**
Bishop Gurdon Ct. HU13: Hess 1G **53**
Bishop Kempthorne Cl. HU13: Hess 1G **53**
Bishop La. HU1: Hull 2D **44** (4F **5**)
Bishop La. Staith HU1: Hull 2D **44** (4F **5**)
Bishops Cft. HU17: Bev 5D **6**
Bishop Temple Ct. HU13: Hess 5G **41**
Bisley Gro. HU7: Brans 5D **18**
Bittern Cl. HU4: Hull 6C **42**
Blackburn Av. HU15: Brou 6D **36**
Blackfriargate HU1: Hull 3D **44** (5F **5**)
Blackhope Cl. HU7: Brans 1D **18**
Blacksmiths Cl. DN19: Bar H 6E **57**
Blackthorn Ct. HU3: Hull 2A **44** (4A **4**)
Blackthorn La. HU10: Will 1G **41**
Blackwater Way HU7: King 1B **18**
Bladons Wlk. HU10: Kir E 6E **25**
Blaides Staithe HU1: Hull 1D **44** (3G **5**)
Blake Cl. HU2: Hull 6B **28** (1C **4**)
Blandford Cl. HU7: Brans 6E **19**
Blanket Row HU1: Hull 3C **44** (5E **5**)
Blanshards La. HU15: N'th C 2A **34**
Blasket Rd. HU14: N'th F 1F **51**
Blaycourt HU6: Hull 6D **16**
Blaydes St. HU6: Hull 2H **27**
Bleach Yard La. HU17: Bev 3C **6**
Blenheim Rd. HU17: Bev 1F **9**
Blenheim St. HU5: Hull 6G **27**
Blenkin St. HU9: Hull 1E **45** (1H **5**)
Blisland Cl. HU7: Brans 3C **18**
Bloomfield Av. HU5: Hull 6B **26**
Bloomsbury Ct. HU3: Hull 2A **44** (3A **4**)
Blossom Gro. HU8: Hull 4G **19**
Blossom's La. HU15: N'th C 1A **34**
Blucher La. HU17: Bev 5F **7**
Blue Ball Entry *HU12: Hed* *2E 49*
(off George St.)
Blueberry Ct. HU4: Hull 4B **42**
Blundell Cl. HU2: Hull 6B **28**
Blyth Ct. DN18: Bart H 5G **55**
Blythorpe HU6: Hull 4E **17**
Blyth St. HU9: Hull 1E **45** (1H **5**)
Boatswain Cft. HU1: Hull 3C **44** (6D **4**)
Bobbers Staith HU3: Hull 4A **44**
Bodmin Rd. HU7: Brans 2C **18**
Boggle La. HU11: Sproat 3F **23**
Boltby M. HU5: Hull 3D **26**
Bon Accord Rd. HU13: Hess 1F **53**
Bondane HU6: Hull 5D **16**
Bond St. HU1: Hull 1C **44** (2D **4**)
HU12: Hed 3G **49**
Bondyke Cl. HU16: Cott 6F **15**
Bontoft Av. HU5: Hull 5D **26**
Boothferry Rd. HU3: Hull 3C **42**
HU4: Hull 6D **40**
HU13: Hess, Hull 1C **52**
Borella Gro. HU3: Hull 4F **43**
Borodales Rd. HU12: Hed 3D **48**
Borrowdale HU7: Brans 6C **18**
Borthwick Cl. HU7: Brans 6D **12**
Borwick Dr. HU17: Bev 4H **7**
Bossington Cl. HU7: Brans 3D **18**
Boston Ct. HU7: King 2B **18**
Bothwell Gro. HU9: Hull 6E **31**
Boulevard HU3: Hull 2G **43**
Boulevard, The HU12: Hed 1E **49**
Boulevard Unit Factory Est. HU3: Hull 4H **43**
Boulsworth Av. HU6: Hull 5H **17**
Boulton Gro. HU9: Hull 4H **29**
Bournemouth St. HU5: Hull 4B **28**
Bourne St. HU2: Hull 1C **44** (1E **5**)
Bowes Wlk. *HU5: Hull* *3D 26*
(off Bishop Alcock Rd.)
HU5: Hull *3D 26*
(off Dent Rd.)
Bowlalley La. HU1: Hull 2C **44** (4E **5**)
Bowl Circ. HU9: Hull 3A **30**
Bowmandale DN18: Bart H 4E **55**
Bow Rd. HU14: Welt 4A **38**
HU15: Welt 4A **38**
Boxtree Wlk. HU3: Hull 3H **43**
BP Av. *HU3: Hull (off Clyde St.)* *3E 43*
Brackendale Cl. HU7: Hull 2E **29**
Brackley Cl. HU8: Hull 4E **29**
Bradford Av. HU9: Hull 4F **31**
Bradwell Cl. DN18: Bart H 4D **54**
Braemar Av. HU6: Hull 6G **17**
Braids Wlk. HU10: Kir E 6C **24**
Bramble Gth. HU17: Bev 1E **7**
HU17: Walk 6A **8**
Bramble Hill HU17: Bev 1F **9**
Brambles, The DN19: Bar H 5E **57**
Brandesburton St. HU3: Hull 6G **27**
Brandon Ct. HU8: Hull 5F **29**
Brandon Way HU7: King 1C **18**
Brandsby Gro. HU9: Hull 3F **31**

Bransdale Gro.—Cave La.

Bransdale Gro. HU9: Hull 6A **30**
BRANSHOLME (Bransholme Rd.) 1G **19**
(Goodhart Rd.) 4E **19**
Bransholme Rd. HU7: Brans 2E **19**
BRANTINGHAM 6G **35**
Brantingham Cl. HU16: Cott 6F **15**
Brantingham Rd. HU15: Ello 1C **36**
BRANTINGHAM THORPE 1D **36**
Brantingham Wlk. HU5: Hull 4B **26**
Brazil St. HU9: Hull 6F **29**
Brecon Av. HU8: Hull 5F **29**
Brecon Dr. HU7: King 1C **18**
Brecon St. HU8: Hull 5F **29**
Brendon Av. HU8: Hull 3E **29**
Brent Av. HU8: Hull 6C **20**
Brentwood Av. *HU5: Hull* *6G* ***27***
(off Hardwick Av.)
HU9: Hull *6F* ***29***
(off Brazil St.)
Brentwood Cl. HU15: Brou 6C **36**
Brentwood Vs. *HU3: Hull* *2G* ***43***
(off Perry St.)
HU5: Hull *4H* ***27***
(off Reynoldson St.)
Brereton Cl. HU17: Bev 2D **6**
Bretherdale HU7: Brans 6C **18**
Brevere Rd. HU12: Hed 2F **49**
Brewery Ho. M. *HU17: Bev* *4D* ***6***
(off Walkergate)
Briar Ct. DN19: Gox 4D **58**
Briarfield Rd. HU5: Hull 4E **27**
Briars, The HU13: Hess 5F **41**
Bricknell Av. HU5: Hull 2C **26**
Brickyard Cotts. HU14: N'th F 3E **51**
Brickyard La. HU14: N'th F 1B **50**
Bridge Cl. HU9: Hull 2F **45**
Bridgegate Dr. HU9: Hull 2F **45**
Bridgeman Ho. HU6: Hull 4F **17**
Bridge Rd. HU15: S'th C 4B **34**
Bridges, The DN18: Bart H 5F **55**
Bridles, The DN19: Gox 5E **59**
Bridlington Av. HU2: Hull 5B **28** (1D **4**)
Bridport Cl. HU7: Brans 5F **19**
Brigg Dr. HU13: Hess 5G **41**
Brigg Rd. DN18: Bart H 6F **55**
Brigham Ct. *HU17: Bev* *3E* ***7***
(off Cooper St.)
Brigham Gro. HU9: Hull 5C **30**
Brighton Rd. Ind. Est. HU3: Hull 5E **43**
Brighton St. HU3: Hull 5E **43**
HU4: Hull 5E **43**
Bright St. HU8: Hull 6E **29**
Brimington Rd. HU10: Will 4G **25**
Brimley HU17: Mole 3B **6**
Brindley St. HU9: Hull 4H **29**
Brisbane St. HU3: Hull 3A **44** (5A **4**)
Bristol Rd. HU5: Hull 5B **26**
Britannia Gdns. HU5: Hull 4B **28**
Brixham Ct. HU3: Hull 3F **43**
Brixton Cl. HU8: Hull 1H **29**
Broadacre Pk. HU15: Ello 6F **37**
Broadgate HU17: Walk 2B **8**
Broadland Dr. HU9: Hull 2B **30**
Broad La. Cl. HU16: Cott 5A **16**
Broadley Av. HU10: Anla 2E **41**
Broadley Cl. HU9: Hull 1F **45**
Broadley Cft. HU15: Brou 6F **37**
Broadley Way HU15: Brou 6F **37**
Broad Oak HU11: Bil 6E **21**
Broadstairs Cl. HU8: Hull 5H **19**
Broadstone Cl. HU7: Brans 6F **19**
Broadwaters HU7: King 2A **18**
Broadway Dr. HU9: Hull 3B **30**
Broadway, The HU9: Hull 3A **30**
Brockenhurst Av. HU16: Cott 1C **26**
Brocklebank Ct. HU12: Prest 5E **33**
Brocklesby Cl. HU13: Hess 5H **41**
Brockley Cl. HU8: Hull 6H **19**
Brockton Cl. HU3: Hull 3D **42**
Brodsworth St. HU8: Hull 6F **29**
Bromley St. HU2: Hull 6C **28**
Brompton Cl. HU5: Hull 4D **26**
HU10: Anla 2H **41**
Brompton Ct. HU3: Hull 5A **28**
Bromwich Rd. HU10: Will 6G **25**
Bronte Ct. HU6: Hull 5H **17**
Brookfield Cl. HU7: King 2B **18**
Brooklands HU7: Hull 1F **29**
Brooklands Cl. HU17: Bev 2F **7**
Brooklands Pk. HU16: Cott 6H **15**
Brooklands Rd. HU5: Hull 6D **26**
Brooklyn Av. *HU5: Hull* *3A* ***28***
(off Brooklyn St.)
HU5: Hull *6G* ***27***
(off Perth St.)
Brooklyn St. HU5: Hull 3A **28**
Brooklyn Ter. HU5: Hull 3A **28**
Brooklyn Vs. HU9: Hull 1D **46**
Brookside HU15: Welt 5G **37**
Brook St. HU2: Hull 1B **44** (3B **4**)
Brook Ter. HU15: N'th C 2A **34**
Broomhead Cl. HU8: Hull 5H **19**
BROUGH 6D **36**
Brougham St. HU3: Hull 1E **43**
Brough Rd. HU15: S'th C 4D **34**
Brough Station (Rail) 6C **36**
Broughton Cl. HU9: Hull 3B **30**
Browning Cl. HU3: Hull 6A **28**
Browns Yd. Ind. Est. HU17: Bev 2E **9**
Brucella Gro. HU3: Hull 4F **43**
Brudenell Way HU6: Hull 3D **16**
Brumby's Ter. HU9: Hull 1G **45**
Brumfield Ct. HU17: Bev 3F **7**
Brunslow Cl. HU3: Hull 3D **42**
Brunswick Av. HU2: Hull 6B **28**
HU9: Hull *1F* ***45***
(off Franklin St.)
Brunswick Gro. HU13: Hess 6F **41**
Brunswick Ter. *HU8: Hull* *5F* ***29***
(off Durham St.)
Buccaneer Way HU15: Brou 6D **36**
Buckingham St. HU8: Hull 5E **29**
(not continuous)
Buckland Cl. HU8: Hull 5D **20**
Bude Rd. HU7: Brans 3B **18**
Budforth La. DN19: Bar H 4H **57**
Budworth Pk. HU7: King 2A **18**
Bull Pasture HU15: S'th C 4C **34**
Burbage Av. HU8: Hull 2F **29**
Burcott Gth. HU4: Hull 5A **42**
Burdale Cl. HU9: Hull 3C **30**
Burdale Wlk. HU16: Cott 2H **25**
Burden Cl. HU17: Bev 3F **7**
Burden Rd. HU17: Bev 3E **7**
Burden St. HU1: Hull 2B **44** (3C **4**)
HU2: Hull 2B **44** (3C **4**)
Burdon Cl. HU10: Will 1G **41**
Burgate DN18: Bart H 3F **55**
Burgess Ct. *HU17: Bev* *3E* ***7***
(off Goths La.)
Burleigh St. HU8: Hull 6F **29**
Burlington Rd. HU8: Hull 1G **29**
Burma Dr. HU9: Hull 6C **30**
Burnaby Cl. HU17: Bev 2D **6**
Burnby Cl. HU5: Hull 4B **26**
Burney Cl. HU17: Bev 3D **6**
Burnham Rd. DN18: Bart H 6H **55**
HU4: Hull 5A **42**
Burniston Rd. HU5: Hull 4D **26**
Burnsalls Rd. HU12: Hed 2D **48**
Burrill La. HU15: Brant 6G **35**
Burrill M. HU5: Hull 3D **26**
Burrs, The HU15: Brou 6C **36**
Burslem St. HU2: Hull 6B **28**
Burton Constable Cvn. Pk. HU11: Burt C 1E **23**
Burton Constable Rd. HU11: Sproat 1F **23**
Burton Rd. HU16: Cott 1G **25**
HU17: Mole 2B **6**
Bush Cl. HU4: Hull 5C **42**
Bushey Pk. HU7: King 2A **18**
Butcher Row HU17: Bev 4E **7**
Buttercup Cl. HU9: Hull 6G **29**
Butterfly Mdws. HU17: Bev 2D **6**
Butt Field Rd. HU13: Hess 1F **53**
Butt La. HU17: Bev (not continuous) 6D **6**
Butts Rd. DN18: Bart H 3E **55**
Buxton Vs. *HU9: Hull* *6G* ***29***
(off Rosmead St.)
Bylands Ct. HU9: Hull 6H **29**
Byron St. HU8: Hull 4G **29**
Bywell Wlk. HU9: Hull 6E **31**

C

Cadeleigh Cl. HU7: Brans 4D **18**
Cadogan Av. *HU3: Hull (off Cadogan St.)* *3G* ***43***
Cadogan Gro. HU3: Hull 3G **43**
Cadogan St. HU3: Hull 3G **43**
Caistor Rd. DN18: Bart H 4F **55**
Caldane HU6: Hull 4D **16**
Caldberg M. HU5: Hull 3D **26**
Calderdale HU7: Brans 5C **18**
Calder Gro. HU8: Hull 6D **20**
Calder Sq. HU15: Brou 6F **37**
Caledon Cl. HU9: Hull 1E **31**
Caledonia Pk. HU9: Hull 3E **45** (5H **5**)
Calthorpe Gdns. *HU3: Hull* *3E* ***43***
(off Newington St.)
Calthorpe St. HU3: Hull 3G **43**
Calvert La. HU4: Hull 1C **42**
Calvert Rd. HU5: Hull 6C **26**
Cambeak Cl. HU7: Brans 2C **18**
Camberwell Way HU8: Hull 1B **30**
Camborne Gro. HU8: Hull 3E **29**
Cambrian Av. *HU9: Hull* *6G* ***29***
(off Holland St.)
Cambridge Ct. HU13: Hess 5F **41**
Cambridge Gro. HU9: Hull 5A **30**
Cambridge Rd. HU13: Hess 5G **41**
Cambridge St. HU3: Hull 2A **44** (4A **4**)
Camden St. HU3: Hull 3G **43**
Camelford Cl. HU7: Brans 3C **18**
Camerton Gro. HU9: Hull 4A **30**
Cam Gro. HU8: Hull 6D **20**
Camilla Cl. HU9: Hull 3D **44** (5G **5**)
Campbell Ct. HU9: Hull 4B **30**
HU13: Hess *6F* ***41***
(off Hourne, The)
Campbell St. HU3: Hull 3A **44**
Camperdown HU11: Bil 6E **21**
Campion Av. HU4: Hull 6A **42**
Canada Dr. HU16: Cott 1F **25**
Canberra St. HU3: Hull 3A **44** (5A **4**)
Canning St. HU2: Hull 2B **44** (3B **4**)
Cannon St. HU2: Hull 6C **28**
Canongate HU16: Cott 5A **16**
Canons Health Club 4B **44** (6B **4**)
Canon Tardrew Ct. HU13: Hess 1G **53**
Canopias Cl. HU3: Hull 4F **43**
Canterbury Cl. HU17: Bev 1E **9**
Canterbury Dr. HU8: Hull 5H **19**
Capital Pk. HU17: Bev 4H **7**
Capstan Rd. HU6: Hull 4H **17**
Captain's Wlk. HU1: Hull 3B **44** (6C **4**)
Carden Av. HU9: Hull 4D **30**
Cardigan Av. *HU3: Hull* *1E* ***43***
(off De La Pole Av.)
HU5: Hull *5B* ***28***
(off Fenchurch St.)
Cardigan Rd. HU3: Hull 1D **42**
Carew St. HU3: Hull 1E **43**
Carisbrooke Av. *HU3: Hull* *1E* ***43***
(off De La Pole Av.)
HU5: Hull *3H* ***27***
(off Manvers St.)
HU8: Hull *5E* ***29***
(off Montrose St.)
HU16: Cott 6A **16**
Carisbrooke Vs. *HU5: Hull* *4G* ***27***
(off Reynoldson St.)
Carlam La. HU7: Waw 5C **12**
Carlisle Av. HU3: Hull 3G **43**
Carlton Av. *HU5: Hull* *4G* ***27***
(off Reynoldson St.)
HU9: Hull 1B **46**
Carlton Ct. HU17: Bev 4D **6**
Carlton Ri. HU17: Bev 2F **9**
Carlton St. HU3: Hull 4E **43**
Carlton Vs. *HU3: Hull (off Greek St.)* *3F* ***43***
HU5: Hull (off Goddard Av.) *4H* ***27***
Carnaby Gro. HU6: Hull 1D **26**
Carnegie St. HU3: Hull 2F **43**
Carnoustie Cl. HU8: Hull 3F **29**
Carol Dickson Ct. HU3: Hull 3H **43**
Caroline Pl. HU2: Hull 1C **44** (1D **4**)
Caroline's Pl. HU16: Skid 4C **14**
Caroline St. HU2: Hull 6C **28** (1D **4**)
Carperby M. HU5: Hull 3C **26**
Carr Cl. HU17: Bev 4F **7**
Carrington Av. *HU3: Hull* *1E* ***43***
(off De La Pole Av.)
HU5: Hull *3H* ***27***
(off Manvers St.)
HU16: Cott 6A **16**
Carrington St. HU3: Hull 3G **43**
Carr La. HU1: Hull 2B **44** (4C **4**)
HU10: Will 5E **25**
Carroll Pl. HU2: Hull 1D **44** (2F **5**)
Carr Rd. HU17: Mole 1C **6**
Carr St. HU2: Hull 6C **28**
Carter Dr. HU17: Bev 1D **6**
Cartmell Ct. HU9: Hull 4D **30**
Cartwright La. HU17: Bev 6C **6**
Castle Ct. DN18: Bart H 4F **55**
HU16: Cott 1E **25**
Castle Dr. HU15: S'th C 3C **34**
Castledyke Sth. DN18: Bart H 4F **55**
Castledyke W. DN18: Bart H 3E **55**
Castle Farm Ct. HU15: S'th C 3C **34**
Castleford Gro. HU9: Hull 5F **31**
Castle Grn. HU16: Cott 6F **15**
Castle Gro. *HU5: Hull* *6F* ***27***
(off Perth St. W.)
Castle Hall HU7: Brans 3E **19**
CASTLE HILL HOSPITAL 1E **25**
Castlehill Rd. HU7: Brans (not continuous) 4F **19**
Castle Ri. HU15: S'th C 3C **34**
Castle Rd. HU16: Cott 1D **24**
Castle St. HU1: Hull 3C **44** (5C **4**)
Castle Way HU13: Hess 2F **53**
Castlton Av. HU5: Hull 3D **26**
Catford Cl. HU8: Hull 1H **29**
Cathedral Cl. HU17: Bev 1F **9**
Catherine Gro. *HU3: Hull* *3G* ***43***
(off Carrington St.)
Catherine McAuley Cl. HU6: Hull 2H **27**
Catherine St. DN18: Bart H 3F **55**
HU2: Hull 6C **28** (1E **5**)
Catterick M. HU5: Hull 3C **26**
Caughey St. HU2: Hull 1A **44** (2A **4**)
Caukeel La. HU16: Cott (not continuous) 5A **16**
Causeway, The HU17: Bev 4E **7**
Cautley M. *HU12: Hed* *2E* ***49***
(off St Augustine's Ga.)
Cave By-Pass HU15: S'th C 5D **34**
Cave Cres. HU16: Cott 6F **15**
Cave La. HU15: Elle 6C **34**

A-Z Hull 63

Glencoe Av.—Hawthorn Ri.

Glencoe Av. *HU3: Hull (off Clyde St.)* *3E 43*
Glencoe St. HU3: Hull 2E 43
Glencoe Vs. *HU9: Hull* *6G 29*
(off New Bridge Rd.)
Glencourt HU6: Hull 6D 16
Glendale Cl. HU10: Kir E 5D 24
Gleneagles Cres. DN19: New H 2A 58
Gleneagles Pk. HU8: Hull 5A 20
Glenfell Cl. HU7: Hull 1G 29
Glenfield Dr. HU10: Kir E 5C 24
Glenhall Ri. DN19: Bar H 5E 57
Glenham Dr. HU10: Will 6G 25
Glenrock Pk. HU15: Brou 5C 36
Glen, The HU10: Kir E 5C 24
HU17: Bev 6G 7
Glenwood Cl. HU8: Hull 3F 29
Glenwood Dr. HU4: Anla 2A 42
Globe M. *HU17: Bev* *4D 6*
(off Sow Hill Rd.)
Gloucester Rd. HU10: Will 4F 25
Gloucester St. HU4: Hull 5D 42
Goathland Cl. HU3: Hull 2F 43
Goble Cl. DN18: Bart H 5G 55
Godbold Cl. HU17: Bev 4F 7
Goddard Av. HU5: Hull 4F 27
Goddard Cl. DN18: Bart H 5D 54
Godman's La. HU10: Kir E 1C 40
Goldcrest Cl. HU7: Brans 4G 19
Golden Ct. HU9: Hull 3B 30
Golden Gro. HU11: Bil 6E 21
Golf Links Dr. HU15: Brou 5C 36
Golf Links Rd. HU6: Hull 1D 26
Goodfell Rd. HU17: Bev 2F 7
Goodhand Cl. DN18: Bart H 5H 55
Goodhart Rd. HU7: Brans 4E 19
Goodmanham Way HU16: Cott 6F 15
Goodrich Cl. HU2: Hull 5B 28
Goodwin Pde. HU3: Hull 3A 44 (5A 4)
Goodwood Cl. HU17: Bev 2D 6
Gordan Pk. HU16: Cott 6B 16
Gordon Av. HU3: Hull 4F 43
HU9: Hull (off Rensburg St.) *5G 29*
Gordon St. HU3: Hull 3G 43
Gorsedale HU7: Brans 5B 18
Gorthorpe HU6: Hull 4F 17
Gorton Rd. HU10: Anla, Will 1F 41
Gosport Wlk. HU4: Hull 4H 41
Gothenburg Way HU7: Hull 6B 18
Goths La. HU17: Bev 3E 7
Gouldesborough Ct. HU5: Hull 3H 27
Goulton St. HU3: Hull 5H 43
Gower Rd. HU4: Hull 5A 42
GOXHILL 5C 58
Goxhill Rd. DN19: Bar H 5G 57
Goxhill Station (Rail) 5C 58
Grafton St. HU5: Hull 4H 27
Graham Av. *HU3: Hull (off Airlie St.)* *3G 43*
HU4: Hull 6A 42
Grammar School Rd. HU5: Hull 4D 26
Grammar School Yd. HU1: Hull 3C 44 (4E 5)
Grampian Way HU7: Brans 6D 12
Granary Ct. HU15: Ello 3E 37
Grandale HU7: Brans 5B 18
Grange Av. DN18: Bart H 4E 55
Grange Cl. HU2: Hull 6C 28
Grange Cres. HU10: Anla 2F 41
Grange Dr. HU16: Cott 5H 15
Grange La. HU14: N'th F 2E 51
HU17: Mole 1E 7
Grange Pk. HU14: Swan 5F 39
HU15: Brou 5D 36
Grange Pk. La. HU10: Will 4C 24
Grange Rd. HU9: Hull 3E 31
HU12: Thorn 6H 49
Grangeside Av. HU6: Hull 1E 27
Grange Way HU17: Bev 1B 6
Grantchester Cl. HU5: Hull 5B 26
Grantham Av. HU7: King 1C 18
Grantley Gro. HU9: Hull 4D 30
Granville Av. *HU3: Hull* *3E 43*
(off Clyde St.)
HU5: Hull *4G 27*
(off Reynoldson St.)
Granville Gro. *HU3: Hull* *3F 43*
(off Greek St.)
HU5: Hull *4B 28*
(off Folkstone St.)
Granville St. HU3: Hull 2F 43
Granville Vs. *HU5: Hull* *4B 28*
(off Sculcoats La.)
Grape La. *HU12: Hed* *2F 49*
(off Baxter Ga.)
Grasby Rd. HU8: Hull 2B 30
Grassam Cl. HU12: Prest 5F 33
Grassdale Pk. HU15: Brou 6C 36
Grassington Cl. HU7: Brans 1C 18
Gravel Pit Rd. DN18: Bart H 4B 54
Grayburn Ct. HU17: Bev 4D 6
Grayburn La. HU17: Bev 5D 6
Great Field La. HU9: Hull 6D 30
Gt. Field La. HU9: Hull 6E 31
Gt. Gutter La. HU10: Will 5A 24
Gt. Gutter La. (East) HU10: Will 4D 24
Gt. Gutter La. (West) HU10: Will 5B 24
Gt. Hornton St. HU3: Hull 3H 43
Gt. Passage St. HU1: Hull 3B 44 (5B 4)
Gt. Thornton St. HU3: Hull 2A 44 (4A 4)
Gt. Union St. HU9: Hull 1D 44 (2G 5)
Greek St. HU3: Hull 3E 43
Green Acres HU10: Kir E 2D 40
Greenacres HU14: Swan 3H 39
Green Cl. HU6: Hull 6E 17
Greendale Ct. HU16: Cott 1F 25
Greenfield HU5: Hull 4B 26
Greenfield Gth. HU6: Hull 3G 17
Greenfields DN19: Gox 5D 58
Greengate La. DN19: Gox 5D 58
Greenhow Cl. HU8: Hull 5H 19
Green Island HU11: Bil 1F 31
Green La. DN18: Bart H 4G 55
DN19: Bar H 5F 57
HU2: Hull 6C 28
HU10: Will 2C 24
HU13: Hess 1H 53
HU14: Welt 1A 50
HU16: Cott 6F 15
HU16: Skid, Will 1C 24
Green Marsh Rd. HU12: Thorn 6G 49
Green Rd. HU12: Hed 3D 48
Greens La. HU7: Waw 4A 12
Greenstiles La. HU14: Swan 3H 39
Green, The HU9: Hull 6H 29
HU11: Sproat 2F 23
HU14: Swan 3F 39
Greenway DN18: Bart H 3G 55
HU4: Hull 4D 42
Green Way HU13: Hess 2F 53
Greenways HU14: N'th F 6E 39
Greenway, The HU4: Hull 2B 42
Greenwich Av. HU9: Hull 2D 30
Greenwood Av. HU6: Hull 1D 26
HU17: Bev 4F 7
Greenwood Gdns. HU17: Bev 1E 7
Grenville Bay HU11: Bil 6E 21
Greville Rd. HU12: Hed 2G 49
Greyfriars Cres. HU17: Bev 5C 6
Greygarth Cl. HU7: Brans 6C 12
Greylees Av. HU6: Hull 4G 17
Greystone Av. HU5: Hull 1D 42
Grey St. HU2: Hull 1A 44 (1A 4)
Griffin Rd. HU9: Hull 3D 30
Grimscott Cl. HU7: Brans 3B 18
Grimston Rd. HU10: Anla 2H 41
Grimston St. HU1: Hull 1C 44 (2E 5)
Grindell St. HU9: Hull 6G 29
Grinton Av. HU5: Hull 6G 27
Grizedale HU7: Brans 5C 18
Grosmont Cl. HU8: Hull 5H 19
Grosvenor Pl. HU17: Bev 6C 6
Grosvenor St. HU3: Hull 6A 28 (1A 4)
Grove Cl. HU17: Bev 3E 7
GROVEHILL 5H 7
Grove Hill HU13: Hess 1F 53
Grovehill Ind. Est. HU17: Bev 5H 7
Grovehill Rd. HU17: Bev 4E 7
Grove Ho. HU10: Anla 2G 41
Grove Ho. Vw. HU5: Hull 3A 28
Grove Pk. HU17: Bev 3D 6
Grove St. HU5: Hull 5A 28
Grove, The DN19: Bar H 5E 57
HU8: Hull 3F 29
Grundale HU10: Kir E 2D 40
Guildford Av. HU8: Hull 2G 29
Guildford Cl. HU17: Bev 1F 9
Guildhall Rd. HU1: Hull 2C 44 (3E 5)
Guillemot Cl. HU4: Hull 6C 42
Gullane Dr. HU6: Hull 3G 17
Guy Gth. HU12: Hed 2G 49
Guy's Cres. HU8: Hull 1B 30

H

Hackforth Wlk. HU5: Hull 2C 26
Hackness Gro. HU5: Hull 6C 26
Haddon St. HU3: Hull 4E 43
Hadleigh Cl. HU2: Hull 5B 28
Haggs La. HU10: Will 3E 25
Haldane Ct. HU4: Hull 6C 42
Haldenby Ct. HU14: Swan 4F 39
Hales Cres. HU12: Hed 3D 48
Hales Entry HU9: Hull 2F 45
Haller St. HU9: Hull 6H 29
Hallgarth Way HU17: Bev 5E 7
Hallgate HU16: Cott 6H 15
Halliwell Cl. HU9: Hull 6F 31
Hall Pk. HU14: Swan 3H 39
Hall Rd. HU6: Hull 4D 16
HU11: Sproat 2F 23
Halls Ct. DN18: Bart H 5H 55
Hall St. HU2: Hull 1A 44 (1A 4)
Hall Wlk. HU15: Welt 4G 37
HU16: Cott 6B 16
HU17: Walk 5A 8
Haltemprice Crematorium HU10: Will 3D 24
Haltemprice Leisure Cen. 1F 41
Haltemprice St. HU3: Hull 3E 43
Halyard Cft. HU1: Hull 3C 44 (6D 4)
Hambledon Cl. HU7: Brans 6E 19
Hambling Dr. HU17: Bev 1D 6
Hamburg Rd. HU7: Hull 1D 28
Hamilton Dr. HU8: Hull 6A 20
Hamling Way HU4: Hull 6C 42
Hamlyn Av. HU4: Hull 1D 42
Hamlyn Dr. HU4: Hull 2D 42
Hammersmith Rd. HU8: Hull 1A 30
Hammond Rd. HU17: Bev 3F 7
Hampshire St. HU4: Hull 5D 42
Hampstead Ct. HU3: Hull 5A 28
Hampston Cl. HU6: Hull 5F 17
Hamshaw Ct. HU3: Hull 4H 43
Hands-on History Mus. 2C 44 (4E 5)
Hanley Rd. HU5: Hull 3C 26
Hanover Ct. HU1: Hull 2B 44 (4B 4)
HU15: N'th C 2B 34
HU17: Bev 4F 7
Hanover Sq. HU1: Hull 2C 44 (3E 5)
Ha'penny Bri. Way HU9: Hull 3E 45 (5H 5)
Harbour Way HU9: Hull 2F 45
Harcourt Dr. HU9: Hull 6F 29
Hardane HU6: Hull 4D 16
Hardington Cl. HU8: Hull 5C 20
Hardwick Av. HU5: Hull 6G 27
Hardwick St. HU5: Hull 6G 27
Hardys Rd. HU12: Hed 3D 48
Hardy St. HU5: Hull 3H 27
Harewood HU17: Mole 2A 6
Harewood Av. HU9: Hull 3B 30
Hargreave Cl. HU17: Bev 2D 6
Harland Rd. HU15: Ello 4E 37
Harland Way HU16: Cott 4D 14
Harlech Cl. HU7: Brans 5C 12
Harleigh Av. HU7: Hull 1E 29
Harlequin Dr. HU7: King 2C 18
Harlestone Cl. HU8: Hull 1C 30
Harley Av. *HU9: Hull* *6F 29*
(off Brazil St.)
Harley St. HU2: Hull 6B 28
Harlow Cl. HU8: Hull 6D 20
Harome Gro. HU5: Hull 1B 42
Harpham Gro. HU9: Hull 5B 30
Harpings Rd. HU5: Hull 5E 27
Harrier Rd. DN18: Bart H 2G 55
Harrington Ct. HU12: Hed 3G 49
Harrison Cl. HU11: Sproat 2F 23
Harris St. HU3: Hull 3E 43
Harrowdyke DN18: Bart H 4E 55
Harrow St. HU3: Hull (not continuous) 4G 43
Harry's Av. *HU8: Hull* *3E 29*
(off Lorraine St.)
Hartford Wlk. HU8: Hull 5D 20
Harthill Dr. HU3: Hull 3H 43
Hartland Cl. HU7: Brans 4C 18
Hartley Bri. HU9: Hull 2E 45
Hartoft Rd. HU5: Hull 4D 26
Hartsholme Pk. HU7: King 2B 18
Harvest Av. DN18: Bart H 5E 55
Harvest Ct. HU17: Bev 4D 6
Harvest Ri. DN19: Bar H 5E 57
Harwood Ct. HU12: Hed 3F 49
Harwood Dr. HU4: Anla 2A 42
Hase Wlk. *HU13: Hess* *1F 53*
(off Station Rd.)
Haslemere Av. *HU5: Hull* *4A 28*
(off Melwood Gro.)
Hastings Av. *HU5: Hull* *4B 28*
(off Folkstone St.)
Hastings Gro. HU5: Hull 1D 42
Hastings Rd. HU12: Thorn 6G 49
Hatfield Hi-Tech Pk. HU3: Hull 5H 43
Hatfield Wlk. HU8: Hull 5F 29
Hathersage Rd. HU8: Hull 2F 29
Hauxwell Gro. HU8: Hull 1A 30
Havelock St. HU3: Hull 4F 43
Haven Av. HU15: Brou 6C 36
Haven Basin Rd. HU12: Hed 4E 49
Haven Gth. HU12: Hed 2G 49
HU15: Brou 6C 36
Haven Mdw. DN18: Bart H 1E 55
Haven Rd. DN18: Bart H 3E 55
Havenside HU12: Hed 4E 49
Haven Staithes HU12: Hed 3E 49
Haven, The HU9: Hull 2E 45 (4H 5)
HU17: Walk 2C 8
Haverflats Cl. HU5: Hull 5E 27
Hawes Wlk. HU5: Hull 3C 26
Hawkesbury St. HU8: Hull 3H 29
Hawkshead Grn. HU4: Hull 1B 42
Haworth St. HU6: Hull 2H 27
Hawthorn Av. HU3: Hull 2E 43
Hawthorn Ct. HU3: Hull 2E 43
Hawthorne Av HU10: Will 5F 25
Hawthorne Av. HU10: Will 5E 25
Hawthorne Gdns. DN19: Gox 4D 58
Hawthorne Gth. HU17: Bev 1E 7
Hawthorne Ri. HU13: Hess 5C 40
Hawthorn Ga. DN18: Bart H 5G 55
Hawthorn Ri. DN19: Bar H 5E 57

Lealholme Ct.—Market Ct.

Lealholme Ct. HU8: Hull 5H 19
Leame Cl. HU3: Hull 1F 43
Leander Rd. HU9: Hull 3C 30
Leases, The HU17: Bev 5D 6
Lea, The HU15: S'th C 2E 35
Leathley Cl. HU17: Bev 1F 9
Leconfield Cl. HU9: Hull 5E 31
Ledbury Rd. HU5: Hull 4C 26
Leeming Gth. HU7: Brans 3F 19
Lee Smith St. HU9: Hull 1H 45
Lee's Rest Ho's. HU4: Hull 2C 42
Lee St. HU8: Hull 3F 29
Lees Wlk. HU3: Hull 1F 43
Lee Vs. *HU8: Hull (off Lee St.)* *4G 29*
Legard Dr. HU10: Anla 2G 41
Legarde Av. HU4: Hull 2B 42
Legion Cl. HU15: Brou 6D 36
Leicester St. HU3: Hull 6A 28
Leitholm Cl. HU7: Brans 6D 12
LELLEY 1H 33
Lelley Balk HU12: Prest 6H 23
Lelley Rd. HU12: Prest 3D 32
Lenham La. HU1: Hull 2B 44 (4C 4)
Leningrad Rd. HU7: Hull 6C 18
Leonard's Av. *HU3: Hull* *3F 43*
(off Rhodes St.)
Leonards Av. HU5: Hull 3A 28
Leonard St. HU3: Hull 6A 28
Leslie Av. *HU8: Hull* *3D 28*
(off Lorraine St.)
Leura Gro. HU3: Hull 4G 43
Leven Gro. HU9: Hull 4B 30
Levisham Cl. HU6: Hull 6E 17
Levita Av. HU9: Hull 4D 30
Lexington Dr. HU4: Hull 3B 42
Leyburn Av. HU6: Hull 2D 26
Leyland Av. HU9: Hull 5G 29
Liberty La. HU1: Hull 2D 44 (4F 5)
Lichfield Cl. HU2: Hull 6B 28
HU17: Bev 1F 9
Liddell St. HU2: Hull 1B 44 (1C 4)
Lilac Av. HU5: Hull 3H 27
HU8: Hull 4E 29
HU10: Will 5E 25
HU17: Bev 1E 7
Lilac Rd. HU15: Brou 6E 37
Lily Gro. *HU3: Hull (off Greek St.)* *3E 43*
Lime Av. HU10: Will 5F 25
HU15: Brou 6E 37
Limedane HU6: Hull 4E 17
Lime Gro. DN19: Gox 4E 59
Limerick Cl. HU8: Hull (not continuous) 6C 20
Limes, The *HU5: Hull (off Ella St.)* *4G 27*
HU15: S'th C 4B 34
Lime St. HU8: Hull 1D 44 (1F 5)
Lime Tree Av. HU7: Hull 6G 19
HU8: Hull 4F 29
HU13: Hess 1G 53
HU17: Bev 2E 7
Lime Tree La. HU11: Bil 6G 21
Lime Tree Vs. HU7: Hull 6G 19
Lincoln Castle Way DN19: New H 1G 57 & 2A 58
Lincoln Dr. DN18: Bart H 5G 55
Lincoln Grn. HU4: Hull 1B 42
Lincoln St. HU2: Hull 6C 28
Lincoln Way HU17: Bev 2E 9
Linden Av. HU16: Cott 5B 16
Lindengate Av. HU7: Hull 2E 29
Lindengate Way HU7: Hull 1E 29
Linden Gro. *HU3: Hull (off Greek St.)* *3F 43*
HU5: Hull (off Folkstone St.) *4B 28*
Lindsey Pl. HU4: Hull 2C 42
Lingcourt HU6: Hull 5E 17
Lingdale Rd. HU9: Hull 4F 31
Linkfield Rd. HU5: Hull 2D 26
Link Rd. HU16: Cott 1H 25
Link, The HU4: Hull 3B 42
Linnaeus St. HU3: Hull 2H 43
Linnet Dr. HU8: Hull 5G 19
Linthorpe Gro. HU10: Will 6F 25
Linton HU15: Ello 5E 37
Linton Cl. HU17: Bev 6D 6
Lisle Ct. HU1: Hull 2C 44 (4D 4)
Lismore Av. HU9: Hull 3B 30
Lissett Gro. HU6: Hull 5H 17
Lister Ct. HU1: Hull 2D 44 (3G 5)
Lister St. HU1: Hull 3B 44 (6A 4)
Littlebeck Cl. HU3: Hull 1F 43
Lit. Clover HU17: Bev 2E 7
Littlefair Rd. HU9: Hull 1B 46
Lit. George St. HU8: Hull 6D 28
Littleham Cl. HU7: Brans 4E 19
Lit. Mason St. HU2: Hull 1D 44 (2F 5)
Littlemoor Cl. HU15: N'th C 2B 34
Lit. Queen St. HU1: Hull 2B 44 (3C 4)
Lit. Reed St. HU2: Hull 1C 44 (2D 4)
Lit. Weighton Rd. HU16: Skid 4A 14
HU17: Walk 6A 8
Lit. Wold La. HU15: S'th C 3E 35
Littondale HU7: Brans 5B 18
HU15: Ello 5F 37
Liverpool St. HU3: Hull (not continuous) 4F 43
Livingstone Rd. HU13: Hess 2F 53
Lizzie's Av. *HU3: Hull* *3E 43*
(off Rhodes St.)
Loatley Grn. HU16: Cott 1B 26
Lock Keepers Ct. HU9: Hull 2F 45
Lockton Gro. HU5: Hull 6C 26
Lockwood Dr. HU17: Bev 1D 6
Lockwood Rd. HU17: Bev 1C 6
Lockwood St. HU2: Hull 6C 28
Lodge Av. DN18: Bart H 5G 55
Lodge Cl. HU13: Hess 1G 53
HU15: Ello 3E 37
Lodge St. HU9: Hull 4H 29
Loftus Gro. HU9: Hull 3F 31
Loganberry Dr. HU4: Hull 4B 42
Logan Cl. HU7: Brans 5F 19
Lois Cres. HU3: Hull 3G 43
Lombard St. HU2: Hull 2B 44 (3B 4)
Lombardy Cl. HU5: Hull 1B 42
Lomond Rd. HU5: Hull 6D 26
Londesborough Barracks *HU3: Hull* *2A 44*
(off Londesborough St.)
Londesborough St. HU3: Hull 1H 43 (2A 4)
Londesborough St. Bus. Cen. HU3: Hull 2H 43
Longcroft Pk. HU17: Mole 3B 6
Longdales La. HU11: Coni 2F 21
Longden St. HU3: Hull 1F 43
Long Dr. HU10: Kir E 6A 24
Longford Gro. HU9: Hull 4F 31
Long La. HU17: Bev 6E 7
Longmans La. HU16: Cott 6A 16
Lonsdale St. HU3: Hull 2F 43
Lord Roberts Rd. HU17: Bev 5E 7
Lords La. DN19: Bar H 5F 57
Lorenzo Way HU9: Hull 4A 30
Lorne Cl. HU2: Hull 6C 28
Lorraine St. HU8: Hull 3D 28
Lothian Way HU7: Brans 6D 12
Louis Dr. HU5: Hull 6A 26
Louis Pearlman Cen. HU3: Hull 4H 43
Louis St. HU3: Hull 6H 27
Lovat Cl. HU3: Hull 3A 44 (6A 4)
Love La. HU12: Hed 3E 49
HU15: S'th C 2D 34
Loveridge Av. HU5: Hull 4F 27
Lowdale Cl. HU5: Hull 5D 26
Lowerdale HU15: Ello 5E 37
Lower Mdws. DN18: Bart H 3G 55
Low Farm Rd. HU11: Bil 3E 21
Lowfield Ct. HU10: Anla 2G 41
Lowfield Ho. *HU10: Anla* *2G 41*
(off Lowfield Rd.)
Low Field La. HU14: Welt 2A 50 & 6H 37
(not continuous)
Lowfield Rd. HU10: Anla 3F 41
HU17: Bev 1E 7
Lowgate HU1: Hull 2D 44 (3F 5)
HU7: Hull 6G 19
Lowgate Cl. HU7: Hull 6G 19
Lowland Cl. HU7: Brans 4G 19
Low Mill La. HU15: N'th C 2A 34
Low St. HU14: N'th F 1E 51
Lowther St. HU3: Hull 2F 43
Loxley Grn. HU4: Hull 1A 42
Loxley Way HU15: Brou 6F 37
Loyds Cl. HU15: S'th C 4B 34
Loyd St. HU10: Anla 2G 41
Lucian Wlk. HU4: Hull 6H 41
Luck La. HU12: Prest 4D 32
Lulworth Av. HU4: Hull 5H 41
LUND 5G 7
Lund Av. HU16: Cott 6F 15
Lunds, The HU10: Kir E 2D 40
Lunedale Cl. HU8: Hull 5H 19
Lunn's Cres. DN18: Bart H 5E 55
Lurk La. *HU17: Bev (off Hallgarth Way)* *5E 7*
Luthers Ri. HU10: Will 4D 24
Luton Rd. HU5: Hull 6E 27
Lymington Gth. HU4: Hull 5H 41
Lyndhurst Av. HU16: Cott 6C 16
Lyndhurst Cl. HU17: Bev 4G 7
Lynmouth Cl. HU7: Brans 3D 18
Lynngarth Av. HU16: Cott 6B 16
Lynton Av. HU4: Hull 5A 42
HU5: Hull (Chanterlands Av.) 6F 27
HU5: Hull (Perth St. W.) 6F 27
Lynwood Av. HU10: Anla 2F 41
Lynwood Gro. *HU5: Hull (off Goddard Av.)* *4H 27*
Lyric Cl. HU3: Hull 3H 43
Lytham Dr. HU16: Cott 1C 26
Lythe Av. HU5: Hull 2C 26

M

Mable's Vs. *HU9: Hull (off Holland St.)* *6G 29*
Mace Vw. HU17: Bev 6E 7
Machell St. HU2: Hull 1C 44 (1E 5)
McKinley Av. *HU3: Hull* *3G 43*
(off Albermarle St.)
Macon Av. *HU5: Hull (off Minton St.)* *3A 28*
Madeley St. HU3: Hull 4H 43
Madison Gdns. HU5: Hull 5F 27
Madoline Gro. *HU9: Hull* *6G 29*
(off Estcourt St.)
Madron Cl. HU7: Brans 4E 19
Mafeking Gro. *HU3: Hull* *3E 43*
(off Seymour St)
Magdalen Ct. HU12: Hed 2G 49
Magdalen Ga. HU12: Hed 2E 49
Magdalen La. HU12: Hed 2F 49
Magnolia Ct. HU3: Hull 3H 43
Maiden Ct. HU7: Brans 3G 19
Main Rd. HU11: Bil, Sproat 6E 21
HU12: Hed, Paul, Thorn 4E 49 & 5F 49
HU14: Welt 1A 50
Main St. HU2: Hull 5C 28
HU7: Waw 4A 12
HU10: Will (not continuous) 3D 24
HU11: Coni 1G 21
HU12: Paul 6A 48
HU12: Prest 4E 33
HU14: Swan 3G 39
HU15: Elle 6D 34
HU15: Ello 4D 36
HU16: Skid 4B 14
Maisons De Dieu HU17: Bev 4D 6
Majestic Ct. HU9: Hull 3B 30
Maldon Dr. HU9: Hull 2F 45
Malham Av. HU4: Hull 2B 42
Mallard Cl. HU17: Bev 2D 6
Mallard Rd. HU9: Hull 2C 30
Mallards Reach HU16: Cott 4B 16
Mallin Lodge HU9: Hull 3B 30
Mallyan Cl. HU8: Hull 5H 19
Malmo Rd. HU7: Hull 1B 28
Malm St. HU3: Hull 2G 43
Malpas Cl. HU7: Brans 3C 18
Maltby La. DN18: Bart H 3E 55
Maltings, The HU17: Bev 4F 7
Maltkiln Rd. DN18: Bart H 2E 55
Malton Rd. HU17: Mole 2A 6
Malton St. HU9: Hull 1D 44 (1G 5)
Malvern Av. HU3: Hull 3F 43
HU5: Hull (off Ella St.) *4H 27*
Malvern Cres. HU5: Hull 4C 26
Malvern Rd. HU5: Hull 4C 26
Manchester Sq. DN19: New H 2A 58
Manchester St. HU3: Hull 4F 43
(not continuous)
Mancklin Av. HU8: Hull 1G 29
Manderville Cl. HU12: Hed 3F 49
Manet Rd. HU8: Hull 5F 29
Manilla La. DN18: Bart H 1E 55
Manor Cl. HU11: Sproat 2F 23
HU17: Bev 3D 6
Manor Ct. HU10: Kir E 1A 40
Manor Dr. HU15: Ello 4E 37
Manorfields HU10: Kir E 1A 40
Manor Gth. HU16: Skid 4A 14
Manorhouse La. HU17: Walk 5A 8
Manor Ho. St. HU1: Hull 3B 44 (6C 4)
Manor La. DN19: Bar H 4F 57
DN19: Gox 4C 58
Manor Pk. HU12: Prest 4F 33
HU17: Bev 3D 6
Manor Rd. HU5: Hull 6A 26
HU12: Prest 4E 33
HU12: Thorn 6H 49
HU14: Swan 4F 39
HU15: N'th C 1A 34
HU17: Bev 4D 6
Manor St. HU1: Hull 2C 44 (3E 5)
Manor Way HU10: Anla 2G 41
Mansfield Pk. HU5: Hull 3G 27
Manston Gth. HU7: Brans 3F 19
Manvers St. HU5: Hull 3H 27
Maple Av. HU10: Will 6G 25
Maple Cl. HU5: Hull 1B 42
Maple Dr. HU17: Bev 2E 7
Maple Gro. HU8: Hull 4F 29
HU13: Hess 5C 40
Maple Leaf Ct. HU16: Cott 1G 25
Maple Pk. HU12: Hed 1F 49
Maple St. HU5: Hull 4A 28
Maplewood Av. HU5: Hull 1H 41
Mappleton Gro. HU9: Hull 4B 30
Marbury Pk. HU7: King 2B 18
Marchant Cl. HU17: Bev 1C 6
Mardale Av. HU9: Hull 3E 31
Mareham Av. *HU3: Hull (off Ena St.)* *2G 43*
MARFLEET 1C 46
Marfleet Av. HU9: Hull 1C 46
Marfleet La. HU9: Hull 2B 30
(not continuous)
Margaret Gro. HU13: Hess 1G 53
Margaret St. HU3: Hull 6A 28
Marina Ct. HU1: Hull 3C 44 (5E 5)
Marina Recreation Cen. 3B 44 (6C 4)
Marin Ct. HU17: Bev 5G 7
Marine Av. HU14: N'th F 3D 50
Mariners Cl. HU9: Hull 2F 45
Mariners Ct. HU17: Bev 5F 7
Marine Wharf HU1: Hull 3C 44 (6C 4)
Maritime Ho. HU3: Hull 5H 43
Market Ct. HU15: S'th C 3D 34

Market Grn. HU16: Cott.	6A **16**
(off King St.)	
Market Hill HU12: Hed	2E **49**
Market La. DN18: Bart H	4F **55**
Market Pl. DN18: Bart H	4F **55**
DN19: Bar H.	5F **57**
HU1: Hull (Sth. Church Side)	4E **5**
HU1: Hull (Garrison Rd.)	3D **44** (5F **5**)
HU12: Hed	2E **49**
HU15: S'th C	3D **34**
Marlborough Av. HU4: Hull	5D **42**
(off Hampshire St.)	
HU5: Hull	6F **27**
HU13: Hess	6E **41**
Marlborough Ter. HU2: Hull	1B **44** (1B **4**)
Marlowe St. HU3: Hull	4F **29**
Marmaduke St. HU3: Hull	4H **43**
Marne St. HU5: Hull	6F **27**
Marsdale HU7: Brans	5C **18**
Marsden Landing	
HU6: Hull	4A **18**
Marshall Av. HU10: Will.	6F **25**
HU12: Prest.	6E **33**
Marshall St. HU3: Hull	4H **27**
Marsh Dr. HU17: Bev.	6D **6**
Marshington Cl. HU3: Hull.	1F **43**
Marsh La. DN18: Bart H	2F **55**
DN19: Bar H, New H	1D **56** & 3A **58**
(not continuous)	
Marske Wlk. HU5: Hull	3D **26**
Martin Cl. HU9: Hull	3C **30**
Martin's Cl. DN19: Bar H	4F **57**
Martin St. HU17: Bev	5G **7**
Marton Gro. HU6: Hull	1E **27**
Marvel St. HU9: Hull	1E **45** (2H **5**)
Marydene Dr. HU6: Hull	1H **27**
Masons Ct. DN18: Bart H	5D **54**
Mason St. HU2: Hull	1C **44** (2E **5**)
Maspin Cl. HU7: King	2B **18**
Massey Cl. HU3: Hull	3G **43**
Massey St. HU3: Hull	4F **43**
Mast Dr. HU9: Hull	2G **45**
Matlock Vs. HU9: Hull	6G **29**
(off Estcourt St.)	
Mattocks La. HU12: Hed	1F **49**
Maulson Dr. HU11: Bil.	6H **21**
Maurice Av. HU3: Hull	4D **28**
Maxim Ct. HU3: Hull	3H **43**
Maxwell St. HU8: Hull	4D **28**
Maybury Rd. HU9: Hull	3A **30**
Maye Gro. HU5: Hull	4B **28**
(off Folkestone St.)	
HU5: Hull	6F **27**
(off Perth St. W.)	
HU8: Hull	5E **29**
(off Dansom La. Nth.)	
HU8: Hull	1G **5**
Mayfair Ct. HU5: Hull	4A **28**
Mayfield Av. HU3: Hull	6H **27**
(off Mayfield St.)	
Mayfield St. HU3: Hull	6H **27**
Mayfield Vs. HU9: Hull	6H **27**
(off Rosmead St.)	
Mayfield Wlk. HU3: Hull	6H **27**
May Gdns. HU7: Hull.	2D **28**
May Gro. HU13: Hess	6E **41**
Mayland Av. HU5: Hull	6H **25**
Mayland Dr. HU16: Cott.	6F **15**
May St. HU5: Hull	3A **28**
May Ter. HU5: Hull	3A **28**
Maythorpe Cl. HU3: Hull	1F **43**
May Tree Av. HU8: Hull	4F **29**
Mayville Av. HU8: Hull	3D **28**
Meadley Ct. HU17: Bev.	4H **7**
Meadow Bank HU17: Bev	1E **7**
Meadowbank Rd. HU3: Hull	1D **42**
Meadow Cl. DN19: Gox.	3D **58**
Meadow Dr. DN18: Bart H.	5G **55**
Meadow Gth. HU6: Hull	3G **17**
Meadows, The HU6: Wood	2F **17**
HU7: Brans	5B **18**
HU10: Kir E	6A **24**
HU15: S'th C	5B **34**
HU17: Bev.	6G **7**
Meadow Vale HU9: Hull	6G **29**
(off Estcourt St.)	
Meadow Wlk. HU14: Swan	3G **39**
Meadow Way HU16: Cott	1G **25**
HU17: Walk	5C **8**
Mead St. HU8: Hull	1G **29**
Mead Wlk. HU4: Hull.	2B **42**
Meaux Rd. HU7: Waw	1C **12**
HU17: Waw	1C **12**
Mechanic La. HU3: Hull	3A **44** (6A **4**)
Meden Av. HU15: Brou	6F **37**
Medina Rd. HU8: Hull	1D **30**
Medlar Dr. HU15: Brou	6F **37**
Megabowl Bowling Alley	5G **43**
Megson Way HU17: Walk	2B **8**
Melbourne Ho. HU1: Hull	5B **4**
Melbourne St. HU5: Hull	3H **27**
Melrose Av. HU3: Hull	3E **43**
(off Rhodes St.)	

Melrose Cres. HU3: Hull	3F **43**
(off Greek St.)	
Melrose Pk. HU17: Bev	5E **7**
Melrose St. HU3: Hull	3E **43**
Melrose Vs. HU5: Hull	4H **27**
(off Chesnut Av.)	
MELTON	6B **38**
Melton Bottom HU14: Welt	6A **38**
Meltonby Av. HU5: Hull	4B **26**
Melton Flds. HU14: N'th F.	1B **50**
Melton Old Rd. HU14: Welt.	6A **38**
Melton Rd. HU14: N'th F	1D **50**
Melville St. HU1: Hull	3B **44** (5B **4**)
Melwood Gro. HU5: Hull	4A **28**
Mendip Cl. HU3: Hull	3H **43**
Mere Flats HU14: Swan	4G **39**
Mere Way HU14: Swan	3G **39**
Merlin Cl. HU8: Hull	5G **19**
Merrick St. HU9: Hull	1E **45**
Merryman Gth. HU12: Hed	3E **49**
Mersey St. HU8: Hull	5F **29**
Mersey Vs. HU9: Hull	6H **29**
(off Rosmead St.)	
Merton Gro. HU9: Hull	5A **30**
Mews, The HU3: Hull	3H **43**
Mickley Gro. HU9: Hull	4D **30**
Middleburg St. HU9: Hull	6G **29**
Middledyke La. HU16: Cott.	4C **16**
Middle Gth. Dr. HU15: S'th C	3D **34**
Middlegate Cl. DN19: Bar H	5E **57**
Middleham Cl. HU9: Hull	6H **29**
Middlehowe Grn. HU17: Walk	5A **8**
Middlehowe Rd. HU17: Walk	5A **8**
Middle La. HU12: Hed	3E **49**
HU12: Prest.	4C **32**
HU17: Bev *(off Morton La.)*	4E **7**
Middlemarsh Cl. HU7: Hull.	2E **29**
Middle Rd. HU17: Hull.	2D **30**
Middlesex Rd. HU8: Hull	1A **30**
Middleton Av. HU9: Hull	5G **29**
(off Rensburg St.)	
Middleton Cl. HU17: Bev.	3F **7**
Middleton Ct. HU5: Hull	6H **27**
Middleton St. HU3: Hull	6H **27**
Middleton Vs. HU3: Hull *(off Clyde St.)*	3E **43**
Midgley Cl. HU3: Hull	3H **43**
Midland St. HU1: Hull	2B **44** (4B **4**)
Midmere Av. HU7: Brans	5E **19**
Midway Gro. HU4: Hull	4D **42**
MILE HOUSE	4G **29**
Milestone Ct. DN18: Bart H	4F **55**
HU15: N'th C	2A **34**
Milford Gro. HU9: Hull	5F **31**
Millbeck Bank HU15: S'th C	6A **34**
Mill Beck Ct. HU16: Cott	5A **16**
Mill Beck La. HU16: Cott	5A **16**
Millbrook Way DN18: Bart H.	5G **55**
Milldane HU6: Hull	4F **17**
Miller's Wlk. HU5: Hull	4E **27**
Millfields DN18: Bart H	5E **55**
Millfields Way DN19: Bar H	5E **57**
MILL HILL (West End)	4D **34**
Mill Hill HU15: Elle	6D **34**
(Elloughton)	4D **36**
Millhouse Woods La. HU16: Cott	4A **16**
Mill La. DN19: Bar H	5E **57**
DN19: Gox.	3D **58**
HU10: Kir E	6E **15**
HU15: Ello	4D **36**
HU15: N'th C	1A **34**
HU15: N'th C	1A **34**
HU16: Cott	5G **15**
HU17: Bev	3E **7**
Mill La. Bus. Pk. HU17: Bev	4E **7**
Mill La. Ct. HU17: Bev *(off Mill La.)*	4E **7**
Mill La. W. HU15: Brou, Ello	5C **36**
Millport Dr. HU4: Hull	6A **42**
Mill Ri. HU14: Swan	4E **39**
HU16: Skid	4C **14**
Mill Rd. HU11: Sproat	2F **23**
HU14: Swan	4D **38**
HU16: Cott, Skid	5D **14**
Mill St. HU2: Hull	2B **44** (3B **4**)
Mill Vw. Rd. HU17: Bev.	5F **7**
Mill Wlk. HU16: Cott	1B **26**
Millway HU15: N'th C	1A **34**
Milson Cl. DN18: Bart H	4E **55**
Minehead Rd. HU7: Brans	3D **18**
Minerva Ter. HU1: Hull	3C **44** (6E **5**)
Minnie's Gro. HU3: Hull	6H **27**
(off Mayfield St.)	
HU3: Hull	1F **43**
(off Walton St.)	
HU3: Hull	3E **43**
(off Beilby St.)	
Minster Av. HU17: Bev.	5E **7**
Minster Cl. HU3: Hull	1H **29**
Minster Ct. HU17: Bev	5D **6**
(off Minster Moorgate)	
Minster Moorgate HU17: Bev	5D **6**
Minster Moorgate W. HU17: Bev	5D **6**
Minster Yd. Nth. HU17: Bev	5E **7**
Minster Yd. Sth. HU17: Bev	5E **7**

Mintfields Rd. HU17: Bev	4F **7**
Minton St. HU5: Hull	3A **28**
Mint Wlk. HU17: Bev	6E **7**
Mirfield Gro. HU9: Hull	4D **30**
Mitcham Rd. HU8: Hull	1B **30**
Mizzen Rd. HU6: Hull	4H **17**
Moat Hill HU10: Anla	2G **41**
Moffat Cl. HU8: Hull	2F **29**
MOLESCROFT	2C **6**
Molescroft Av. HU17: Bev	2C **6**
Molescroft Dr. HU17: Bev	2C **6**
Molescroft M. HU17: Bev	2B **6**
Molescroft Pk. HU17: Bev	2B **6**
Molescroft Rd. HU17: Bev.	2B **6**
Mollison Rd. HU4: Hull	5H **41**
Mollison Rd. W. HU4: Hull	5H **41**
Monic Av. HU13: Hess.	5G **41**
Monkton Cl. HU15: Ello	5F **37**
Monkton Ct. HU16: Cott	1G **25**
Monkton Wlk. HU16: Cott	6D **20**
Monmouth St. HU4: Hull	5D **42**
Mons St. HU5: Hull	6F **27**
Montcalm Wlk. HU16: Cott	1G **25**
Montreal Av. HU3: Hull	3G **43**
(off Albermarle St.)	
Montreal Cres. HU16: Cott	1F **25**
Montrose Av. HU3: Hull	3E **43**
(off Seymour St.)	
HU8: Hull	5E **29**
Montrose St. HU8: Hull	5E **29**
Moorbeck Cl. HU8: Hull	2E **27**
Moorfoot Cl. HU7: Brans	1D **18**
Moor Grn. HU4: Hull	1A **42**
Moorhouse Rd. HU5: Hull	6A **26**
Moorings, The HU14: N'th F	3E **51**
Moorlands, The HU15: S'th C	4A **34**
Moor La. HU17: Walk	4A **8**
Moors La. HU15: S'th C	4A **34**
More Hall Dr. HU8: Hull	5G **19**
Moreton Bay HU11: Bil	1F **31**
Morgan Way DN19: New H	1G **57**
Morley's La. HU17: Bev	4D **6**
(off Walkergate)	
Morley St. HU8: Hull.	4D **28**
Morley's Vs. HU9: Hull	5F **29**
(off Sherburn St.)	
Morpeth St. HU3: Hull	1A **44** (1A **4**)
Morrill St. HU9: Hull	5G **29**
Morris Rd. HU9: Hull.	2D **42**
Mortimer Av. HU10: Anla	2G **41**
Mortlake Cl. HU8: Hull	1H **29**
Morton La. HU17: Bev.	4D **6**
Morton St. HU3: Hull	1H **43**
Moseley Hill HU11: Bil	6H **21**
Motherwell Cl. HU9: Hull	2F **29**
Mt. Airy La. HU15: S'th C	4D **34**
Mount Av. DN18: Bart H.	4E **55**
HU13: Hess	6E **41**
Mount Pleasant DN19: New H.	3A **58**
HU8: Hull.	5D **28**
HU9: Hull	6F **29**
Mt. Vernon HU1: Bil.	6F **21**
Mount Vw. HU14: N'th F	6E **39**
Moy Ct. HU6: Hull	6F **17**
Muirfield Pk. HU5: Hull	5F **27**
Mulberry Cl. HU9: Hull	5C **30**
Mulcourt HU6: Hull	5E **17**
Mulgrave St. HU8: Hull	6D **28**
Mullion Cl. HU7: Brans	5F **19**
Multi-sport Indoor Cen.	1F **43**
Munroe Cl. HU3: Hull	2F **29**
Murray Cres. HU16: Cott.	1G **25**
Murrayfield Rd. HU5: Hull.	5E **27**
Mus. of Army Transport	5F **7**
Muston Av. HU16: Cott	1H **25**
Muswell Cl. HU8: Hull.	1B **30**
Mylor Cl. HU7: Brans	3D **18**
Myrtle Av. HU3: Hull	4H **43**
HU9: Hull	1E **45**
(off Williamson St.)	
Myrtle Gro. HU3: Hull	3F **43**
(off Springburn St.)	
HU8: Hull.	3D **28**
(off Lorraine St.)	
Myrtle Vs. HU3: Hull	6H **27**
(off Spring Bank.)	
Myrtle Way HU15: Brou	6E **37**
Mytongate HU1: Hull	3B **44** (5C **4**)
Myton St. HU1: Hull	2B **44** (4C **4**)

N

Naburn St. HU3: Hull	4F **43**
Nairn Cl. HU6: Hull	4G **17**
Nalton Ct. HU16: Cott	1H **25**
Nandike Cl. HU10: Anla	2G **41**
Napier Cl. HU3: Hull	3D **6**
Narrow La. HU14: N'th F	1E **51**
Narvick Rd. HU9: Hull	1B **28**
Nashcourt HU6: Hull	5E **17**
National Av. HU5: Hull.	4E **27**

Navenby Gro.—Packman La.

Navenby Gro. HU7: King . . . 1C 18
Navigation Way HU9: Hull . . . 2F 45
Naylors Row HU9: Hull . . . 1E 45 (2H 5)
Neasden Cl. HU8: Hull . . . 1H 29
NEAT MARSH . . . 4H 31
Neat Marsh Rd. HU12: Prest . . . 5H 31
Neatshead Gth. HU7: Brans . . . 3F 19
Nectan Cl. HU3: Hull . . . 4F 43
Needham Cl. *HU17: Bev (off Bielby Dr.)* . . . *4G 7*
Nelson Ct. HU1: Hull . . . 3C 44 (6E 5)
Nelson Rd. HU5: Hull . . . 1A 42
Nelson St. HU1: Hull . . . 3C 44 (6E 5)
Nelson Vs. HU8: Hull . . . 1G 5
Nepean Gro. *HU3: Hull (off Tyne St.)* . . . *4G 43*
Neptune St. HU3: Hull . . . 4A 44
Nesfield Av. *HU5: Hull* . . . *6F 27*
(off Perth St. W.)
Ness Cl. HU12: Prest . . . 4E 33
Ness La. HU12: Prest . . . 4E 33
Nestlings, The HU8: Hull . . . 2G 29
Nestor Gro. HU9: Hull . . . 1D 30
Netherton Rd. HU4: Hull . . . 4A 42
Neville Av. HU17: Bev . . . 3F 7
Neville Cl. HU3: Hull . . . 3A 44 (6A 4)
Neville Gth. HU12: Hed . . . 2F 49
Newbald Gro. HU6: Hull . . . 6E 17
Newbald Rd. HU17: Bev, Walk . . . 6A 6 & 1A 8
Newbald Way HU16: Cott . . . 6F 15
Newbegin HU17: Bev . . . 4D 6
New Bridge Rd. HU9: Hull . . . 6F 29
Newby Cl. HU7: King . . . 1B 18
New Cleveland St. HU8: Hull . . . 6D 28 (1G 5)
Newcomen St. HU9: Hull . . . 5G 29
New Cross St. HU1: Hull . . . 2C 44 (3D 4)
NEW FIELD . . . 3B 48
Newfield La. HU15: S'th C . . . 4A 34
Newfinkle Ct. HU16: Cott . . . 6H 15
New Garden St. HU1: Hull . . . 1C 44 (2D 4)
Newgate St. HU16: Cott . . . 6A 16
New George St. HU2: Hull . . . 1C 44 (1E 5)
NEW HOLLAND . . . 2A 58
New Holland Rd. DN19: Bar H . . . 5G 57
New Holland Station (Rail) . . . 1A 58
Newholme Cl. HU6: Hull . . . 1E 27
Newington Av. HU4: Hull . . . 3C 42
Newington St. HU3: Hull . . . 4E 43
NEWLAND . . . 3A 28
Newland Av. HU5: Hull . . . 4H 27
Newland Ct. HU5: Hull . . . 3H 27
Newland Gro. HU5: Hull . . . 3H 27
Newland Homes, The HU6: Hull . . . 2H 27
NEWLAND PARK . . . 3H 27
Newland Pk. HU5: Hull . . . 3F 27
Newland Pk. Av. HU6: Hull . . . 2G 27
Newlands Science Pk. HU6: Hull . . . 1G 27
Newlands, The HU5: Hull . . . 3H 27
Newlyn Cl. HU7: Brans . . . 5F 19
HU13: Hess . . . 6H 41
New Michael St. HU1: Hull . . . 3B 44 (5B 4)
New Nth. Bri. Ho. HU1: Hull . . . 1D 44 (2F 5)
Newport DN18: Bart H . . . 3E 55
Newport Cl. HU3: Hull . . . 3A 44
Newport Rd. HU15: N'th C . . . 2A 34
New Princes Av. HU12: Hed . . . 2D 48
New Rd. HU12: Hed . . . 2D 48
HU15: Brant . . . 1D 36
Newsham Gth. HU4: Anla . . . 3A 42
Newstead Av. *HU5: Hull* . . . *6F 27*
(off Newstead St.)
Newstead St. HU5: Hull . . . 6F 27
New St. HU3: Hull . . . 3E 43
Newtondale HU7: Brans . . . 5C 18
Newton Dr. HU17: Bev . . . 6D 6
Newton St. HU3: Hull . . . 4G 43
Newton Thorpe Cotts. HU14: Swan . . . 3F 39
Newton Vs. *HU9: Hull* . . . *6G 29*
(off Estcourt St.)
Newtown Ct. HU9: Hull . . . 6H 29
Newtown Sq. HU9: Hull . . . 1H 45
NEW VILLAGE . . . 6C 16
New Village Rd. HU16: Cott . . . 5B 16
New Wlk. HU14: N'th F . . . 2E 51
New Walk HU17: Bev . . . 3C 6
New Walkergate HU17: Bev . . . 4D 6
Nicholas Ct. DN18: Bart H . . . 5D 54
Nicholson Cl. HU17: Bev . . . 4G 7
Nicholson Ct. HU16: Cott . . . 6H 15
Nicholson Dr. DN18: Bart H . . . 5G 55
Nicholson St. HU5: Hull . . . 4B 28
Nidderdale HU7: Brans . . . 5B 18
Nightingale Cl. HU17: Walk . . . 2C 8
Nithdale Gdns. HU5: Hull . . . 4B 28
Nith Gro. HU8: Hull . . . 5D 20
Noddle Hill Way HU7: Brans . . . 2D 18
Nolloth Cres. HU17: Bev . . . 4E 7
Nolloth Wlk. *HU17: Bev* . . . *4E 7*
(off Nolloth Cres.)
Nordale Cl. HU8: Hull . . . 5H 19
Nordham HU15: N'th C . . . 1A 34
Norfolk Bank La. HU15: Elle . . . 6A 34
Norfolk St. HU2: Hull . . . 1B 44 (1B 4)
HU17: Bev . . . 3C 6
Norland Av. HU4: Hull . . . 1B 42
Norland Ct. *HU13: Hess* . . . *1H 53*
(off Hull Rd.)
Norman Cl. DN18: Bart H . . . 4G 55
Normandy Av. HU17: Bev . . . 2D 8
Normanton Ri. HU4: Hull . . . 1B 42
Nornabell Dr. HU17: Bev . . . 1D 6
Nornabell St. HU8: Hull . . . 5F 29
Norrison Av. HU6: Hull . . . 4H 17
Nth. Bar Within HU17: Bev . . . 4D 6
Nth. Bar Without HU17: Bev . . . 3C 6
NORTH CARR . . . 2E 19
NORTH CAVE . . . 2A 34
Nth. Church Side HU1: Hull . . . 2C 44 (4E 5)
Nth. Country Ct. HU9: Hull . . . 5H 29
Northcroft Dr. HU8: Hull . . . 5H 19
Northdale Pk. HU14: Swan . . . 3G 39
North Dr. HU10: Anla . . . 2F 41
HU14: Swan . . . 3G 39
Northella Dr. HU4: Hull . . . 2D 42
NORTH END . . . 2E 59
North End DN19: Gox . . . 4D 58
Northern Gateway HU9: Hull . . . 1B 46
NORTH FERRIBY . . . 1E 51
NORTHFIELD . . . 6G 41
Northfield HU14: Swan . . . 3G 39
Northfield Av. HU13: Hess . . . 5F 41
Northfield Cl. HU15: S'th C . . . 4B 34
Northfield Rd. HU3: Hull . . . 2E 43
HU11: Coni . . . 1G 21
HU17: Bev . . . 2B 6
Northfield Vs. *HU9: Hull* . . . *6G 29*
(off Rosmead St.)
Northgate HU13: Hess . . . 6F 41
HU16: Cott . . . 5H 15
HU17: Walk . . . 5B 8
Northgate Ho. HU16: Cott . . . 5A 16
Northgate Pl. HU13: Hess . . . 6F 41
North Lincolnshire & Humberside Sailing Club . . . 1A 56
NORTH MOOR . . . 3C 16
North Moor La. HU16: Cott . . . 1C 16
Northmoor La. HU16: Cott . . . 5B 16
Northolme Circ. HU13: Hess . . . 6F 41
Northolme Cres. HU13: Hess . . . 6F 41
Northolme Rd. HU13: Hess . . . 6F 41
Northolt Cl. HU8: Hull . . . 6H 19
Northorpe Cl. HU9: Hull . . . 5D 30
North Point Shop. Cen. HU7: Brans . . . 4E 19
North Rd. HU4: Hull . . . 2D 42
Northstead Cl. HU10: Will . . . 4F 25
North St. DN19: Bar H . . . 4F 57
HU2: Hull . . . 1B 44 (2B 4)
HU10: Anla . . . 2F 41
Northumberland Av. HU2: Hull . . . 5C 28
Northumberland Ct. HU2: Hull . . . 5C 28
North Walls HU1: Hull . . . 2D 44 (3F 5)
Northwood Cl. HU8: Hull . . . 6D 20
Northwood Dr. HU13: Hess . . . 5D 40
Norton Gro. HU4: Hull . . . 4C 42
Norton St. HU17: Bev . . . 5D 6
Norwich Ct. HU17: Bev . . . 1F 9
Norwood HU17: Bev . . . 4D 6
Norwood Cl. HU10: Anla . . . 1F 41
Norwood Ct. HU17: Bev . . . 3E 7
Norwood Dale HU17: Bev . . . 4D 6
Norwood Far Gro. HU17: Bev . . . 2E 7
Norwood Gro. HU17: Bev . . . 2D 6
Norwood St. HU3: Hull . . . 1H 43
Noseley Way HU7: King . . . 1C 18
Novello Gth. HU4: Anla . . . 4A 42
Nunburnholme Av. HU14: N'th F . . . 2D 50
Nunburnholme Pk. HU5: Hull . . . 1A 42
Nun La. HU12: Prest . . . 4E 33
Nunnery Cotts. HU12: Prest . . . 6H 23
Nunnery Wlk. HU15: S'th C . . . 4B 34
Nunnington Cl. HU5: Hull . . . 4G 27
Nurseries, The HU17: Bev . . . 2C 6
Nursery Cl. DN18: Bart H . . . 3G 55
HU12: Thorn . . . 5F 49
Nursery Ct. HU15: Brou . . . 6E 37
Nursery Gdns. HU17: Bev . . . 6D 6
Nursery Wlk. HU16: Cott . . . 6C 16
Nuttles La. HU12: Prest . . . 2H 33

O

Oak Av. HU3: Hull . . . 1E 43
HU10: Will . . . 5E 25
HU15: Ello . . . 5E 37
Oak Cl. HU11: Sproat . . . 2F 23
HU17: Bev . . . 2F 7
Oakdale Av. HU10: Will . . . 6F 25
Oakdene HU16: Cott . . . 6A 16
Oak Dr. HU5: Hull . . . 1A 42
Oakfield Ct. HU6: Hull . . . 2E 27
Oak Gro. DN19: Bar H . . . 6E 57
HU12: Hed . . . 2D 48
Oak Hill HU10: Will . . . 4D 24
Oakington Gth. HU7: Brans . . . 4F 19
Oaklands Dr. HU10: Will . . . 5D 24
HU13: Hess . . . 5E 41
Oakland Vs. *HU5: Hull* . . . *4G 27*
(off Reynoldson St.)
Oak Rd. HU6: Hull . . . 6H 17
Oaksley Carr HU17: Wood . . . 1B 10
Oak Sq. HU7: Waw . . . 3A 12
Oak Tree Cl. HU17: Bev . . . 2C 6
Oaktree Dr. HU8: Hull . . . 5G 19
Oak Tree Dr. HU17: Bev . . . 2C 6
Oak Tree Est. HU12: Prest . . . 5E 33
Oakwell Gro. HU8: Hull . . . 5E 29
Oakwood Cl. HU5: Hull . . . 1H 41
Oban Av. *HU3: Hull* . . . *1E 43*
(off De La Pole Av.)
HU9: Hull . . . 3B 30
Occupation La. HU14: Swan . . . 1G 39
Ocean Blvd. HU9: Hull . . . 2E 45 (4H 5)
Octagon, The HU10: Will . . . 6E 25
Odeon Cinema (HU1) . . . 4B 44 (6C 4)
(HU3) . . . 6F 43
Old Annandale Rd. HU10: Kir E . . . 6D 24
Oldbeck Rd. HU17: Bev . . . 4H 7
Old Ct. HU17: Bev . . . 3C 6
Old Dairy DN19: Bar H . . . 5G 57
Oldfield Av. HU6: Hull . . . 6H 17
Oldgate HU16: Skid . . . 3B 14
HU17: Skid . . . 1B 14
Old La., The HU14: N'th F . . . 2E 51
Old Manor Lawns HU17: Bev . . . 5E 7
Old Pond Pl. HU14: N'th F . . . 3E 51
Old Stables, The HU17: Bev . . . 4C 6
Oldstead Av. HU6: Hull . . . 6E 17
Old Waste HU17: Bev . . . 4D 6
Olivier Ct. HU4: Hull . . . 5D 42
On Hill HU14: Swan . . . 3G 39
Onyx Gro. HU3: Hull . . . 4F 43
Orchard Cen., The HU13: Hess . . . 1F 53
Orchard Cl. DN18: Bart H . . . 5G 55
DN19: Bar H . . . 6E 57
HU10: Anla . . . 1G 41
HU17: Bev . . . 3C 6
Orchard Ct. HU15: S'th C . . . 3D 34
Orchard Cft. HU16: Cott . . . 4A 16
Orchard Dr. HU13: Hess . . . 1F 53
Orchard Gth. HU17: Bev . . . 2C 6
Orchard Pk. & North Hull Enterprises
HU6: Hull . . . 3D 16
Orchard Pk. Rd. HU6: Hull . . . 4D 16
(Hall Rd.)
HU6: Hull . . . 4C 16
(Middledyke La.)
Orchard Rd. HU4: Anla . . . 3A 42
HU16: Skid . . . 4B 14
Orchard, The HU9: Hull . . . 2C 30
Orchard Vw. *HU15: N'th C* . . . *1A 34*
(off Church St.)
Oribi Cl. HU4: Hull . . . 6B 42
Oriel Cl. HU17: Walk . . . 2C 8
Oriel Gro. HU9: Hull . . . 5B 30
Orion Cl. HU3: Hull . . . 3G 43
Orkney Cl. HU8: Hull . . . 5H 19
Ormerod Cres. HU5: Hull . . . 4C 26
Ormerod Rd. HU5: Hull . . . 4C 26
Ormesby Wlk. *HU5: Hull* . . . *3C 26*
(off Sedburgh Av.)
Ormington Vs. *HU9: Hull* . . . *1F 45*
(off Field St.)
Ormonde Av. HU6: Hull . . . 2A 28
Orniscourt HU6: Hull . . . 5E 17
Orpington Vs. *HU9: Hull* . . . *5G 29*
(off Rensburg St.)
Osborne St. HU1: Hull . . . 2B 44 (4B 4)
Oslo Rd. HU7: Hull . . . 6B 18
Osprey Cl. HU6: Hull . . . 4G 17
Ossett Cl. HU8: Hull . . . 5F 29
Oswald Ct. HU5: Hull . . . 4C 26
Otley Cl. HU9: Hull . . . 4D 30
Ottawa Cl. HU16: Cott . . . 1G 25
Otterburn St. HU3: Hull . . . 3F 43
Outer Trinities HU17: Bev . . . 5E 7
Outgang, The HU15: Brant . . . 2B 36
Outlands Rd. HU16: Cott . . . 1C 26
Outram Cl. HU2: Hull . . . 6B 28
Oval, The HU8: Hull . . . 4F 29
HU10: Will . . . 6F 25
HU15: Ello . . . 5E 37
Overland Rd. HU16: Cott . . . 1B 26
Overstrand Dr. HU7: Hull . . . 6G 19
Overton Av. HU10: Will . . . 5F 25
Overton Ct. DN18: Bart H . . . 3F 55
Owbridge Ct. HU1: Hull . . . 2B 44 (4B 4)
Owen Av. HU13: Hess . . . 1H 53
Owthorne Vs. *HU9: Hull (off Rosmead St.)* . . . *6G 29*
Oxenhope Rd. HU6: Hull . . . 5A 18
Oxford Cl. HU17: Bev . . . 1F 9
Oxford St. HU2: Hull . . . 5D 28
Oxmarsh La. DN19: New H . . . 2A 58

P

Pacific Ct. HU1: Hull . . . 4F 5
Packman La. HU10: Kir E . . . 6C 24

Q

St Clements Pl. HU2: Hull	5B 28
St David Cl. HU17: Bev	5E 7
	(off Hallgarth Way)
St David's Cl. HU16: Cott	6B 16
St Edmund's Ct. HU5: Hull	4C 26
St Ellens Ct. HU17: Bev	5E 7
	(off Eastgate)
St Frances Ct. HU5: Hull	4B 26
St George's Av. HU3: Hull	3F 43
St George's Gro. HU3: Hull	2F 43
St George's Rd. HU3: Hull	2F 43
St Georges Ter. HU3: Hull	4G 43
	(off Redbourne St.)
St George's Vs. HU9: Hull	1E 45
St George's Wlk. HU9: Hull	4C 30
St Giles Ct. HU9: Hull	5D 30
St Gile's Cft. HU17: Bev	5D 6
St Hedda's Ct. HU5: Hull	4C 26
St Helena Gdns. HU5: Hull	4B 28
	(off Tunis St.)
St Helen's Dr. HU15: Welt	5G 37
St Hilda St. HU3: Hull	5B 28
St Ives Cl. HU7: Brans	5F 19
St James Cl. HU7: Brans	5G 19
HU12: Hed	3E 49
HU13: Hess	1H 53
St James Ct. HU7: Hull	6G 19
HU9: Hull	2E 45
St James M. HU13: Hess	3F 7
	(off Newlyn Cl.)
St James Reckitt's Village Haven HU8: Hull	5F 29
St James Rd. HU14: Welt	6B 38
St James Sq. HU3: Hull	3A 44 (6A 4)
St James St. HU3: Hull	3A 44 (6A 4)
St Johns Bus. Pk. HU9: Hull	5A 30
St John's Cl. DN19: Gox	5D 58
St John's Cl. HU12: Hed	3E 49
HU17: Bev	2F 9
St John's Ct. HU6: Hull	2A 28
St John's Gro. HU9: Hull	5A 30
St John St. HU17: Bev	5E 7
St John's Wlk. HU13: Hess	6G 41
St Joseph Dr. HU4: Hull	3B 42
St Jude's Ct. HU5: Hull	4C 26
St Julians Wells HU10: Kir E	1E 41
St Katherines Rd. HU15: S'th C	4A 34
St Lawrence Av. HU16: Cott	1G 25
St Leonards Cl. HU12: Hed	3D 48
	(off Draper's La.)
St Leonards Rd. HU5: Hull	4A 28
St Leonard's Rd. HU17: Bev	2B 6
St Luke's Ct. HU10: Will	6G 25
St Lukes St. HU3: Hull	2A 44 (4A 4)
St Margarets Av. HU16: Cott	6F 15
St Margarets Cl. HU16: Cott	6F 15
St Margarets Ct. HU8: Hull	6D 20
St Mark's Sq. HU3: Hull	4A 44 (6A 4)
St Mark's Ter. HU17: Bev	4C 6
St Mark St. HU8: Hull	6D 28
St Martins Av. HU4: Hull	2D 42
St Martin's Ct. HU17: Bev	5D 6
St Martin's Ct. HU4: Hull	2C 42
St Martins Ct. HU12: Thorn	5G 49
St Martin's Rd. HU12: Thorn	6G 49
St Mary's Av. HU5: Hull	2C 26
St Mary's Cl. HU12: Thorn	6G 49
St Marys Cl. HU13: Hess	3D 52
St Mary's Cl. HU15: Ello	3D 36
HU17: Bev	3C 6
St Mary's Dr. HU12: Hed	3G 49
St Marys La. DN18: Bart H	4F 55
St Marys La. HU17: Bev	4D 6
St Marys Mt. HU16: Cott	6B 16
St Mary's Wlk. HU17: Bev	3C 6
St Matthews Ct. HU17: Bev	5E 7
St Matthew St. HU3: Hull	3G 43
St Michael's Cl. DN19: Gox	5D 58
HU16: Skid	4B 14
St Michael's Dr. HU12: Hed	3G 49
St Michael's Mt. HU6: Hull	2H 27
HU14: Swan	3G 39
St Monica's Ct. HU5: Hull	3H 27
St Nicholas Av. HU4: Hull	6B 42
St Nicholas Dr. HU17: Bev	5F 7
St Nicholas Gdns. HU4: Hull	6C 42
St Nicholas Ga. HU12: Hed	3F 49
St Nicholas Rd. HU17: Bev	4F 7
St Ninians Wlk. HU5: Hull	5F 27
St Pancras Cl. HU3: Hull	3H 43
St Paul St. HU2: Hull	6B 28
St Peter's Av. HU10: Anla	1F 41
St Peter's Ct. DN18: Bart H	3E 55
St Peter's Orchard DN18: Bart H	3F 55
St Peter St. HU9: Hull	2D 44 (3G 5)
St Peters Vw. HU11: Bil	6G 21
St Quintins Cl. HU9: Hull	1F 45
Saints Cl. HU9: Hull	4A 30
St Silas St. HU3: Hull	6C 28
St Stephen's Cl. HU10: Will	4D 24
St Stephens Sq. HU1: Hull	2A 44 (3A 4)
St Stephens St. HU1: Hull	2A 44 (3A 4)

St Thomas More Rd. HU4: Anla	4H 41
St Thomas's Grange HU5: Hull	4C 26
St Wilfred's Av. HU3: Hull	3F 43
	(off Greek St.)
Salcey St. HU7: King	1B 18
Salisbury Av. HU3: Hull	3F 43
HU17: Bev	1F 9
Salisbury Gdns. HU5: Hull	3H 27
	(off Raglan St.)
Salisbury St. HU5: Hull	4G 27
HU13: Hess	1F 53
Salisbury Vs. HU9: Hull	6G 29
	(off Holland St.)
Salmon Gro. HU6: Hull	2G 27
Saltash Rd. HU4: Hull	6H 41
Saltburn Av. HU5: Hull	4B 28
	(off Folkstone St.)
Saltburn St. HU3: Hull	4F 43
SALT END	2A 48
Salt End La. HU12: Salt (not continuous)	3H 47
Saltford Av. HU4: Hull	6G 31
Saltgrounds Rd. HU15: Brou	6C 36
Salthouse La. HU1: Hull	2D 44 (3F 5)
Salton Av. HU5: Hull	3D 26
Salthouse Rd. HU8: Hull	6H 19
Saltwell Pk. HU7: King	1B 18
Salvesen Way HU3: Hull	5F 43
Samman Cl. HU10: Anla	2E 41
Samman Rd. HU17: Bev	3F 7
Sample Av. HU17: Bev	3E 7
Sancton Cl. HU5: Hull	5A 28
HU16: Cott	6F 15
Sandale Ct. HU5: Hull	5D 26
Sandfield Dr. HU15: Ello	6E 37
Sandford Cl. HU7: Brans	3C 18
SANDHOLM	1G 7
Sand La. HU15: S'th C	3A 34
Sandlemere Cl. HU3: Hull	3F 43
Sandmoor Cl. HU8: Hull	6C 20
Sandpiper Dr. HU4: Hull	6A 42
Sandringham Cl. HU16: Cott	6H 15
Sandringham Cotts. HU15: Brant	1D 36
	(off Outgang, The)
Sandringham St. HU3: Hull	2F 43
Sandringham Vs. HU3: Hull	2F 43
	(off Wells St.)
Sands Cl. HU14: N'th F	2E 51
Sands La. HU15: Elle	6D 34
HU15: Ello	3D 36
Sandwith Ct. HU17: Bev	3E 7
	(off Goths La.)
Sandycroft Cl. HU5: Hull	5H 25
Sandy Point HU11: Bil	1F 31
Saner's Cl. HU16: Cott	1A 26
Saner St. HU3: Hull	2G 43
Santolina Way HU4: Hull	6B 42
Sapperton Cl. HU7: King	1C 18
Sapphire Gro. HU3: Hull	4F 43
Sargeant Cl. HU12: Hed	3D 48
Saturday Mkt. HU17: Bev	4D 6
	(off Ladygate)
Saunders Cft. HU17: Walk	5A 8
Saunders La. HU17: Walk	5A 8
Savannah Av. HU5: Hull	3A 28
	(off Minton St.)
Savery St. HU9: Hull	5G 29
Savile Cl. HU17: Bev	2D 6
Saville Cl. HU3: Hull	2C 44 (3D 4)
Saville Row HU1: Hull	3D 4
	(off Saville Ct.)
Saville St. HU1: Hull	2C 44 (3D 4)
Savoy Rd. HU8: Hull	2A 30
Sawston Av. HU5: Hull	4B 26
Saxby Rd. HU8: Hull	1B 30
Saxcourt HU6: Hull	5D 16
Saxon Cl. DN18: Bart H	4G 55
Saxondale HU4: Hull	1A 42
Saxon Ri. HU17: Bev	1C 6
Saxon Vs. HU3: Hull	4F 43
Saxon Way HU13: Hess	1G 53
Scaife Cl. HU7: Brans	5F 7
Scaife M. HU17: Bev	5G 7
Scalby Gro. HU5: Hull	6C 26
Scale La. HU1: Hull	2D 44 (4F 5)
Scale La. Staith HU1: Hull	2D 44 (4F 5)
Scampton Gth. HU7: Brans	4F 19
Scarborough St. HU3: Hull	5F 43
Scarrington Cres. HU4: Hull	2A 42
Scarrow Cl. HU3: Hull	1F 43
Schofield Av. HU17: Bev	4F 7
HU17: Wood	2C 10
Schofield Cl. DN19: Bar H	5E 57
School La. DN19: Gox	5D 58
DN19: New H	2A 58
HU10: Kir E	6C 24
HU14: N'th F	2E 51
HU17: Bev (not continuous)	4D 6
School La. M. HU17: Bev	4E 7
School Rd. HU12: Prest	5E 33
School St. HU1: Hull	1B 44 (3C 4)
Schooner Ct. HU4: Hull	5A 42
Schubert Cl. HU9: Hull	3B 30
Scotney Cl. HU2: Hull	5B 28

Scott St. HU2: Hull	1C 44 (1E 5)
Scrubwood La. HU17: Bev (not continuous)	2C 6
SCULCOATES	4B 28
Sculcoates La. HU5: Hull	4A 28
Seafield Av. HU3: Hull	3A 30
Seagran Av. HU13: Hess	5G 41
Seagull Cl. HU4: Hull	6C 42
Seamer Av. HU8: Hull	1G 5
Seaton Gro. HU3: Hull	3D 42
Seaton Rd. HU13: Hess	6G 41
Sedburgh Av. HU5: Hull	3C 26
Sedbury Cl. HU7: King	1B 18
Sedgebrook Gro. HU7: King	1C 18
Sedge Cl. DN18: Bart H	3F 55
Sefton St. HU3: Hull	4G 43
Segrave Gro. HU5: Hull	6C 26
Selby St. HU3: Hull	3F 43
Selina's Cres. HU9: Hull	4G 27
	(off Rosmead St.)
Selkirk St. HU5: Hull	6F 27
Selsey Cl. HU5: Hull	4A 28
Selworthy Cl. HU7: Brans	2D 18
Selwyn Av. HU14: N'th F	2E 51
Sequana Cl. HU9: Hull	2E 45 (4H 5)
Setterwood Gth. HU10: Will	6F 25
Setting Cres. HU5: Hull	4C 26
Setting Rd. HU5: Hull	4C 26
Seven Corners La. HU17: Bev	4C 6
Severndale HU5: Hull	4G 27
	(off Goddard Av.)
Severn Cl. HU8: Hull	5F 29
Severn Vs. HU9: Hull	6H 29
	(off Rosmead St.)
Sewer La. HU1: Hull	3C 44 (5E 5)
Sextant Rd. HU6: Hull	4H 17
Seymour St. HU3: Hull	3E 43
Shadwell Ri. DN18: Bart H	3D 54
Shaftesbury Av. HU3: Hull	2A 30
Shakespear Cl. HU3: Hull	6A 28 (1A 4)
Shannon Rd. HU8: Hull	6D 20
Shardeloes HU11: Bil	1F 31
Sharpe Cl. DN18: Bart H	5E 55
Sharps La. HU17: Walk	6A 8
Sharp St. HU5: Hull	4G 27
Shaw St. HU3: Hull	1E 45 (1H 5)
Shead Grn. HU4: Hull	2B 42
Sheffield Ter. DN19: New H	2A 58
Sheffield Vs. DN19: New H	2A 58
	(off School La.)
Sheldon Cl. HU7: Brans	3E 19
Sheldrake Way HU17: Bev	2E 7
Shelley Av. HU3: Hull	4D 30
Shepherd La. HU17: Bev	2E 9
Shepherds Cl. HU17: Bev	2E 9
	(off Shepherds Lea)
Shepherds Lea HU17: Bev	2E 9
Sherbrooke Av. HU5: Hull	2D 26
Sherburn St. HU9: Hull	5G 29
Sheriff Highway HU12: Hed	3E 49
Sherwood Av. HU5: Hull	6G 27
HU9: Hull	5H 29
Sherwood Cl. HU17: Walk	5C 8
Sherwood Cl. HU11: Bil	1E 31
Sherwood Dr. HU4: Hull	1H 41
Sherwood Gro. HU5: Hull	6F 27
	(off Perth St.)
Shetland Cl. HU8: Hull	5H 19
Shevington Wlk. HU8: Hull	6D 20
Shields Rd. HU12: Hed	2D 48
Shilling Cl. HU7: King	2B 18
Shipley Cl. HU3: Hull	5D 30
Shipton Cl. HU9: Hull	1E 31
Shirethorn Cen. HU2: Hull	1B 44 (2B 4)
Shire Vw. HU17: Walk	6A 8
Shirley Av. HU5: Hull	6F 27
	(off Perth St. W.)
Shopeth Way HU17: Wood	2C 10
Shoreditch Cl. HU8: Hull	1A 30
Shorthill Cft HU17: Bev	6D 6
Short St. HU1: Hull	2A 44 (3A 4)
HU2: Hull	2B 44 (3B 4)
Shorwell Cl. HU8: Hull	6D 20
Shropshire Cl. HU5: Hull	5C 26
Sibelius Rd. HU4: Anla	4A 42
Sicey La. HU17: Wood	6F 11
Sidings Cl. HU15: Brou	6C 36
Sidmouth St. HU5: Hull	3H 27
Sigston Rd. HU17: Bev	2F 7
Silkstone Wlk. HU8: Hull	6F 29
Silsden Av. HU6: Hull	5H 17
Silverdale HU9: Hull	6H 29
	(off Rosmead St.)
Silverdale Rd. HU6: Hull	6H 17
Silver St. DN19: Bar H	6E 57
HU1: Hull	2D 44 (4E 5)
Silvester Sq. HU1: Hull	1C 44 (2D 4)
Silvester St. HU1: Hull	1C 44 (2D 4)
Simpson Cl. DN19: Bar H	5F 57
Simson Ct. HU17: Bev (off Goths La.)	3E 7
Sinclair Cres. HU8: Hull	6A 20
Sinderby Wlk. HU5: Hull	6F 29
Sirius Cl. HU3: Hull	3G 43
Sissons Way HU5: Hull	3B 28

Sister's Cotts.—Swanland Dale

Sister's Cotts. *HU12: Thorn* 6G 49
(off St Mary's Dr.)
Sittingbourne Cl. HU8: Hull 4H 19
Sitwell St. HU8: Hull 6D 28
Skelton Av. HU5: Hull 4D 26
Skern Gro. HU9: Hull 5B 30
SKIDBY 5B 14
Skidby Carr La. HU6: Wood 1C 16
Skidby Gro. HU6: Hull 1E 27
Skidby Windmill & East Riding Mus. of Rural Life 5C 14
Skilgate Cl. HU7: Brans 3D 18
Skillings La. HU15: Brou 6D 36
Skipworth Cl. HU6: Hull 6G 17
Skirbeck Rd. HU8: Hull 1G 29
Sleaford Av. HU9: Hull 4F 31
Sledmere Gro. HU4: Hull 3D 42
Sleightholme Cl. HU7: King 1B 18
Sleights Cl. HU3: Hull 1F 43
Slingsby Cl. HU5: Hull 3C 26
Sloe La. HU17: Bev 6C 6
Smedley Cl. HU17: Bev 5F 7
Smithall Rd. HU17: Bev 1D 6
Snainton Gro. HU5: Hull 6C 26
Snowdon Way HU7: Brans 5C 12
Snowhill Cl. HU7: Brans 6D 12
Snuff Mill La. HU16: Cott 6A 16
(not continuous)
Soffham Cl. HU7: Brans 3C 18
Soff La. DN19: Gox 6F 59
Somerden Rd. HU9: Hull 1F 47
Somerscales St. HU2: Hull 6B 28
Somerset Av. *HU9: Hull* 1F 45
(off Franklin St.)
Somerset St. HU3: Hull 3F 43
Somerville Ct. *HU12: Hed* 3F 49
(off Thorn Rd.)
Sophia Cl. HU2: Hull 6B 28
Sorbus Ct. HU3: Hull 2A 44 (4A 4)
Sorbus Vw. HU5: Hull 1B 42
Sorrel Dr. HU5: Hull 5C 26
Sorrell Cl. HU17: Bev 1F 9
Souhwick Ct. HU17: Bev 1E 9
Soutergate DN18: Bart H 3F 55
South Bridge Rd. HU9: Hull 3D 44 (5G 5)
(not continuous)
Southburn Av. HU5: Hull 1D 42
SOUTH CAVE 3D 34
South Cave Sports Cen. 4C 34
Sth. Church Side HU1: Hull 2C 44 (4E 5)
South Cl. HU6: Hull 6H 17
Southcoates Av. HU9: Hull 4H 29
Southcoates La. HU9: Hull 5G 29
Southcote Cl. HU15: S'th C 3D 34
Southcroft Dr. HU8: Hull 5H 19
Sth. Ella Dr. HU10: Kir E 1E 41
Sth. Ella Way HU10: Kir E 1D 40
SOUTH END 6F 59
Southern Dr. HU4: Hull 3B 42
SOUTH FIELD 2E 53
2G 21
Southfield HU13: Hess 2E 53
South Field Ct. HU16: Cott 1G 25
Southfield Dr. HU14: N'th F 3D 50
HU17: Bev 2F 7
Southfield Rd. HU5: Hull 4F 27
Southgate HU13: Hess 1F 53
Southgate Cl. HU10: Will 4F 25
South Holderness Sports Cen. 6F 33
Sth. Humberside Ind. Est. DN18: Bart H 2G 55
South La. HU13: Hess 1F 53
Sth. Orbital Trad. Pk. HU9: Hull 2F 45
South Ri. HU16: Skid 4C 14
South St. HU1: Hull 2B 44 (3C 4)
HU16: Cott 6H 15
South Vw. HU4: Hull 2A 42
HU9: Hull 5G 29
(off Sherburn St.)
HU12: Hed 2F 49
Southwell Av. HU9: Hull 6F 31
Southwell Cl. HU17: Bev 1F 9
Southwood Av. HU16: Cott 6G 15
Southwood Dr. HU16: Cott 6H 15
Southwood Gdns. HU16: Cott 1G 25
Southwood Rd. HU16: Cott 1G 25
Soutter Ga. HU12: Hed 2E 49
Sovereign Way HU7: King 2A 18
Sow Hill Rd. HU17: Bev 4D 6
Spacemade Pk. HU8: Hull 4D 28
Spark Mill La. HU17: Bev 5F 7
Spark Mill Rd. HU17: Bev 5F 7
Sparkmill Ter. HU17: Bev 5F 7
Speedwell La. HU17: Walk 2C 8
Speeton Gro. HU5: Hull 1C 42
Spencer Cl. HU12: Hed 3E 49
HU16: Cott 6G 15
Spencer Ct. HU3: Hull 2G 43
Spencer St. HU2: Hull 1B 44 (2B 4)
HU17: Bev 4D 6
Spencer Way HU16: Cott 5A 16
Sperrin Cl. HU9: Hull 3B 30
Spicers Rd. HU12: Hed 3D 48
Spindlewood HU15: Ello 3D 36
Spinnaker Cl. HU9: Hull 2F 45
HU12: Hed 3G 49
Spinney Cft. Cl. HU14: N'th F 1D 50
Spinney, The DN19: Bar H 5F 57
HU14: Swan 3G 39
HU16: Cott 1H 25
Spinney Wlk. HU4: Hull 2B 42
Spinney Way HU17: Walk 6B 8
Spire Vw. HU13: Hess 1F 53
Spout Hill HU15: Brant 6H 35
Spring Bank HU3: Hull 6H 27 (1A 4)
Spring Bank W. HU3: Hull 1E 43
HU5: Hull 1A 42
Springbok Cl. HU4: Hull 6C 42
Springburn St. HU3: Hull 3F 43
Springdale Cl. HU9: Hull 6C 30
HU10: Will 6G 25
Springdale Way HU17: Bev 6D 6
Springfield Av. HU15: Ello 5E 37
Springfield Cl. *HU15: Welt* 5G 37
(off Cowgate)
Springfield Ct. HU10: Anla 2H 41
Springfield Dr. HU17: Bev 2F 7
Springfield Rd. HU3: Hull 2E 43
Springfield Vs. *HU3: Hull* 3E 43
(off Pretoria St.)
Springfield Way HU10: Anla 1F 41
Spring Gdns. HU4: Anla 2A 42
HU8: Hull 1G 29
Spring Gdns. E. HU4: Anla 2A 42
Spring Gdns. Sth. HU4: Anla 3A 42
Spring Gdns. W. HU4: Anla 2A 42
Spring Gro. HU3: Hull 1F 43
Springhead Av. HU5: Hull 1H 41
Springhead Gdns. HU5: Hull 1H 41
Springhead La. HU4: Anla 2H 41
HU5: Anla, Hull (not continuous) 1H 41
Springhead Pumping Station (Yorkshire Water Mus.) 1H 41
Spring St. HU2: Hull 1A 44 (2A 4)
Spring Va. HU11: Bil 1E 31
Springville Av. HU13: Hess 6G 41
SPROATLEY 2F 23
Sproatley Rd. HU11: Sproat 6F 23
HU12: Prest, Sproat 4E 33
Spruce Rd. HU1: Hull 3B 44 (6B 4)
Spurn Lightship 3C 44 (5D 4)
Spyvee St. HU8: Hull 1D 44 (1F 5)
Square, The DN19: Gox 5D 58
HU13: Hess 1F 53
Stable La. DN18: Bart H (not continuous) 2D 54
Stafford St. HU2: Hull 6B 28
Staines Cl. HU8: Hull 2B 30
Staithes Rd. HU12: Hed, Prest 1A 48
Stalybridge Av. HU9: Hull 5F 31
Stamford Gro. HU9: Hull 5F 31
Stanbury Rd. HU6: Hull 5H 17
Standage Rd. HU12: Thorn 6G 49
Standidge Dr. HU8: Hull 1B 30
Stanhope Av. HU9: Hull 4H 29
Stanley St. HU3: Hull 1H 43
Stannington Dr. HU8: Hull 6E 21
Stansfield Cl. HU9: Hull 5E 31
Stapleford Cl. HU9: Hull 4F 31
Starboard Av. HU6: Hull 4H 17
Starella Gro. HU3: Hull 4F 43
Startforth Wlk. *HU5: Hull (off Lythe Av.)* 3D 26
Stathers Wlk. HU10: Anla 2G 41
Station Dr. HU5: Hull 5A 28
Station La. HU12: Hed 1E 49
Station Rd. HU12: Prest 5E 33
HU13: Hess 2F 53
HU14: N'th F 2E 51
HU15: Brou 6C 36
HU15: N'th C 2A 34
HU15: S'th C 1C 34
HU16: Cott 5B 16
Station Sq. *HU17: Bev (off Trinity La.)* 4E 7
Station Vw. HU14: N'th F 2E 51
Station Wlk. HU16: Cott 6B 16
Staveley Rd. HU9: Hull 4C 30
Staxton Ct. HU9: Hull 6G 29
Steep Hill HU15: S'th C 2F 35
Steeton Av. HU6: Hull 5H 17
Stembridge Cl. HU9: Hull 5F 31
Stephen Cres. DN18: Bart H 4G 55
Stephenson Cl. HU12: Hed 3G 49
Stephenson Ct. HU5: Hull 4F 27
Stephenson St. HU9: Hull 5H 29
Stephenson's Wlk. HU16: Cott 6C 16
STEPNEY 5A 28
Stepney La. HU5: Hull 5B 28
Stevenson's Way DN18: Bart H 5E 55
Stewart Gth. HU16: Cott 6F 15
Steynburg St. HU9: Hull 5G 29
Stirling St. HU3: Hull 2E 43
Stirling Vs. *HU3: Hull* 2E 43
(off Stirling St.)
Stockbridge Pk. HU15: Ello 3D 36
Stockbridge Rd. HU15: Ello 3C 36
Stockholm Pk. HU12: Hed 3F 49
Stockholm Rd. HU7: Hull 6B 18
HU12: Thorn 6G 49
Stockleigh Cl. HU7: Brans 4C 18
Stocksbridge Av. HU9: Hull 5F 31
Stockwell Gro. HU9: Hull 6F 31
Stockwell La. HU12: Hed 2E 49
Stoke St. HU2: Hull 6B 28
Stonebridge Av. HU9: Hull 5E 31
Stonecarr Ct. HU7: Waw 4A 12
Stone Cl. DN19: Bar H 6F 57
STONEFERRY 2D 28
Stoneferry Pk. HU8: Hull 4D 28
Stoneferry Rd. HU7: Hull 2D 28
HU8: Hull 2D 28
Stonegate Cl. HU8: Hull 5G 19
Stonepit Rd. HU14: Welt 3A 38
HU15: Elle, S'th C 6C 34
HU15: S'th C 5D 34
HU15: Welt (not continuous) 4H 37
Stonesdale HU7: Brans 6C 18
Stones Mt. HU16: Cott 6H 15
Storkhill Rd. HU17: Bev 3F 7
Stornaway Sq. HU8: Hull 5A 20
Story St. HU1: Hull 1B 44 (2C 4)
Stothards La. DN19: Gox 4D 58
Strand Cl. HU2: Hull 6B 28
Stratford Wlk. HU9: Hull 5F 31
Strathcona Av. HU5: Hull 3D 26
Strathcona Vs. HU9: Hull 1C 46
Strathearn St. HU5: Hull 3A 28
Strathmore Av. HU6: Hull 6H 17
Stratton Cl. HU8: Hull 6C 20
Stratton Pk. HU14: Swan 4G 39
Strawberry Gdns. HU9: Hull 1F 45
Strawberry St. HU9: Hull 1E 45 (2H 5)
Strawberry St. Ind Est. HU9: Hull 1E 45
Stray, The HU15: S'th C 2D 34
Streetlife Transport Mus. 2D 44 (3G 5)
Strensall Rd. HU5: Hull 5B 26
Strickland St. HU3: Hull 4H 43
Strines Gro. HU8: Hull 5G 19
Stromness Way HU8: Hull 5A 20
Stroud Cres. E. HU7: Brans 4D 18
Stroud Cres. W. HU7: Brans 4D 18
Studley Ct. HU9: Hull 1F 45
Studley St. HU8: Hull 6E 29
Styles Cft. HU14: Swan 4H 39
Subway St. HU3: Hull 4G 43
Suddaby Cl. HU9: Hull 4A 30
Suffolk St. HU5: Hull 3A 28
Suffolk Ter. HU5: Hull 3A 28
Sullivan Bus. Pk. HU3: Hull 5G 43
Sullivan Rd. HU4: Anla 4A 42
Summercroft Av. DN19: New H 3A 58
Summerdale DN18: Bart H 5E 55
SUMMERGANGS 5G 29
Summergangs Dr. HU12: Thorn 6G 49
Summergangs Rd. HU8: Hull 3F 29
Summergroves Way HU4: Hull 6A 42
Sunbeam Rd. HU4: Hull 3C 42
Sunningdale Rd. HU4: Hull 4E 43
HU13: Hess 6F 41
Sunnybank DN18: Bart H 4D 54
Sunny Bank HU3: Hull 1G 43
Sunny Dene *HU3: Hull* 1E 43
(off De La Pole Av.)
Sunnydene Vs. *HU9: Hull* 6G 29
(off Estcourt St.)
Sunny Gro. *HU5: Hull (off Sharp St.)* 4H 27
Surbiton Cl. HU8: Hull 1A 30
Surrey Gth. HU4: Hull 4A 42
Sussex Cl. HU5: Hull 5C 26
Sutherland Av. HU6: Hull 6G 17
Sutton Cl. HU7: Brans 4E 19
Sutton Ct. HU8: Hull 6H 19
Sutton Fields Ind. Est. HU7: Hull 6B 18
(not continuous)
Sutton Gdns. HU7: Brans 5E 19
Sutton Ho. Rd. HU8: Hull 1G 29
SUTTON INGS 2A 30
SUTTON ON HULL 6G 19
Sutton Rd. HU6: Hull 6H 17
HU7: Hull 6B 18
HU7: Waw 4B 12
HU8: Hull 6B 18
Sutton St. HU3: Hull 1A 44
Sutton Vw. HU8: Hull 3E 29
Sutton Way HU9: Hull 4C 30
Swabys Yd. *HU17: Bev* 4D 6
(off Walkergate)
Swaddale Av. HU10: Will 4G 25
Swainby Cl. HU8: Hull 5G 19
Swaledale HU15: Ello 5F 37
Swaledale Av. HU9: Hull 5H 29
Swale Rd. HU15: Brou 6F 37
Swallowfield Dr. HU4: Hull 6A 42
Swallow Grange HU8: Hull 5G 19
Swallows, The HU16: Cott 4B 16
Swanage Wlk. HU4: Hull 4A 42
Swanella Gro. HU3: Hull 4F 43
Swanfield Rd. HU9: Hull 3D 30
SWANLAND 4G 39
Swanland Butts Cl. HU10: Kir E 2D 40
Swanland Dale
HU14: Kir E, Swan, Welt 1E 39 & 5A 24